A LENTEN

with Jesus Christ and

SAINT FRANCIS DE SALES

Daily Gospel Readings

with

Selections from the Writings

of

St. Francis de Sales

REFLECTIONS AND PRAYERS

BY

REV. ALEXANDER T. POCETTO, O.S.F.S.

WITH ADDITIONAL INTRODUCTORY MATERIAL BY

PETER J. MONGEAU

WELLESLEY, MA
www.ChristusPublishing.com

Christus Publishing, LLC
Wellesley, Massachusetts
www.ChristusPublishing.com

Fr. Alexander T. Pocetto, O.S.F.S. entered the Oblates of St. Francis de Sales in 1945. He obtained an A.B. and M.A. from the Catholic University of America, and was awarded a Ph.D. from the University of Laval, Quebec. He was ordained in 1955. For the past forty-five years, he has been at De Sales University in Center Valley, Pennsylvania, where he was a founding member and served in various leadership positions including Acting President.

Peter J. Mongeau is the Founder and Publisher of Christus Publishing, LLC.

Publisher's Cataloging-in-Publication Data
Pocetto, Alexander T.
   A Lenten Journey with Jesus Christ and Saint Francis de Sales : daily Gospel readings with selections from the writings of St. Francis de Sales : reflections and prayers / by Alexander T. Pocetto ; with additional introductory material by Peter J. Mongeau.
      p. ; cm.

   Includes bibliographical references.
   ISBN: 978-0-9841707-3-9

   1. Lent--Prayers and devotions. 2. Francis, de Sales, Saint, 1567-1622. 3. Francis, de Sales, Saint, 1567-1622--Prayers and devotions. 4. Catholic Church--Prayers and devotions. 5. Oblates of St. Francis de Sales--Prayers and devotions. 6. Prayer books. I. Mongeau, Peter J. II. Title.

BX2170.L4 P63 2010
242/.34   2010932706

Printed and bound in the United State of America

10   9   8   7   6   5   4   3   2   1

Text design and layout by Peri Swan
This book was typeset in Garamond Premier Pro with Snell Roundhand as a display typeface

CONTENTS

ACKNOWLEDGMENTS

The Gospel passages are taken from the *Lectionary for Mass for Use in the Dioceses of the United States of America, second typical edition* © 2001, 1998, 1997, 1986, 1970. Confraternity of Christian Doctrine, Inc., Washington, DC. Used with permission. All rights reserved. No portion of this text may be reproduced by any means without permission in writing from the copyright owner.

The citations from the works of St. Francis de Sales are from *Oeuvres de Saint François de Sales, Edition Complète.* 26 vols. (Annecy: Monastère de la Visitation, 1892–1964). Noted as OEA. The translations are the author's unless otherwise noted.

Francis de Sales, Jane de Chantal, Letters of Spiritual Direction, trans. Sr. Peronne-Marie Thibert, V.H.M., intro. Joseph F. Power, O.S.F.S. and Wendy M. Wright, pref. Henry J. M. Nouwen (New York: Paulist Press, 1988).

Introduction to a Devout Life, trans. with intro. J. K. Ryan (New York: Doubleday, 1966). Noted as IDL.

Lenten Sermons of St. Francis de Sales, trans. by the nuns of the Visitation, ed. Lewis Fiorelli, O.S.F.S. (Rockford, IL: Tan, 1985). With permission of the Sisters of the Visitation of the Rockville, VA monastery. Noted as LS.

Treatise on the Love of God, trans. with intro. J. K. Ryan. 2 vols. (Stella Niagara, NY: De Sales Resource Center, 2007). Noted as TLG. With permission from the De Sales Resources and Ministries.

Reflections and prayers copyright © 2009 Christus Publishing, LLC.

DEDICATION

I dedicate this book to all of my Oblate confreres who have helped me deepen my understanding of our great Salesian heritage by the way they live and joyfully transmit the rich, enduring, and endearing insights of this lovable saint. May this modest contribution to that effort enrich the spiritual lives of all who read it.

REV. ALEXANDER T. POCETTO, O.S.F.S.

AN INVITATION
FROM
ST. FRANCIS
DE SALES

Images of travel and voyages abound in the writings of St. Francis de Sales who encouragingly and alluringly invites those seeking his guidance to travel the road that Jesus himself has so graciously and courageously opened up for us. This he has done by his life, death and resurrection, thereby giving us access to God. It is St. Francis de Sales's thought and ideas that are paraphrased and adapted here to present an enticing invitation to make this Lenten journey in his company and in that of Our Lord. And there are no more alluring words than those of Jesus himself as reflected on by our saint. The words of Jesus that he is "the way, the truth and the life" (Jn 14:6) are to be engraved and impressed in our hearts so deeply that only death can efface them since without Jesus Christ our life is rather death than life. Without the truth that he brings to the world, everything is full of confusion, and if we fail to follow in his footsteps, we will not be able to find the road that leads to heaven. When Jesus tells us that he is the way, the truth and the life, he is making it clear that he himself is the true way: the life-giving and grace-giving way.

To allow God's grace to penetrate our hearts, our saint recommends certain dispositions that we should have as we undertake this Lenten journey. We should have the singleness of purpose of pleasing God in everything we do and not be overly concerned about the difficulties that lie ahead. It is with a gentle, humble and docile heart that we begin so as not to become overly eager and anxious. A receptive heart is open to receive whatever graces and gifts that come our way. We set out with a firm and general purpose to serve God with all our heart and all our life and without worrying about tomorrow. If we concentrate on doing good things during the present day, then tomorrow will take care of itself. This requires that we have a great trust and confidence in the providence of God, who knows what we need, when we need it, and places it within our reach. Like the ancient Israelites, we only collect enough manna for each day, trusting that God will keep supplying us with spiritual nourishment. This attitude makes us aware of how precious and grace-filled each moment is and of the power of living in the "now."

These dispositions readily lead us to appreciate how extraordinary the ordinary everyday occurrences of our lives can be, especially during the Lenten season. This involves walking in the low valleys of the little virtues of simplicity of life, gentleness of heart and poverty of spirit, and practicing such ordinary actions as visiting the sick, serving the poor, consoling the afflicted and similar kindnesses. On these occasions, we will see roses bloom amid thorns, love that bursts forth amid interior and exterior afflictions, and lilies of purity blossom (see *OEA*, 13:92).[1]

To make the journey less burdensome, it is wise at the outset to get rid of excess baggage, of the things that will hinder and inhibit our

---

1. *Oeuvres de Saint François de Sales, Edition Complètes*, 26 vols. (Annecy: Monastère de la Visitation, 1892–1964). Hereafter, OEA. The translations are the author's unless otherwise noted.

progress, causing us to stray from the path that our travel companions tread with us.

It is essentially love of some good or hatred of some evil that gets us stirred up and moving toward what we seek or want to avoid. It is especially love of the Lord Jesus that urges us to make this journey, to sustain and complete it. When this is the driving force that makes us forge ahead, we know and believe that there will be some disconcerting detours. On these occasions, we must not torment our hearts but gently bring them back on track by making spiritual aspirations that continually raise our minds and hearts to God so that they will be fashioned after the heart of Jesus.

This journey is not only for the spiritually robust but particularly for the spiritually handicapped who feel the crushing burden of their humanity with all of its imperfections and shortcomings. Our "handicapped" situation makes us realize all the more how much we are dependent upon God's merciful love and upon one another both to encourage us to undertake this journey and to continue it to its conclusion. It makes us all the more conscious of how Jesus is journeying with us. This assurance will buoy us up when we feel down and moderate our enthusiasm so that we can more effectively tend to the business that is at hand. Just as pilgrims, who from time to time, interrupt their journey, to drink some wine, so Jesus will serve as our wine to give joy to our hearts. In Jesus alone, we will find our rest and refreshment as he urges us to do.

We must not be surprised nor disheartened to see some old bad habits popping up again even though we thought we were rid of them. They are there to remind us that we must always mistrust ourselves and walk in holy fear, not so much fearful of being punished but fearful of not responding promptly and joyfully to God's love as we should.

At times, the sheer volume of the daily duties that face us—getting the children up and dressed for school, making arrangements to drive them to their various activities, driving elderly parents to the doctor's office, trying to do more at work with less—can be a continual martyrdom and hound us like pesky flies as we walk on a hot summer day. It is at these times that we need to have a balance in our lives. Just as a tightrope walker carries a staff to maintain his balance as he performs various precarious maneuvers, so must we firmly hold on to the cross of Our Lord to maintain our spiritual equilibrium. In this way, we will make each step count and go from virtue to virtue.

It is God's grace that makes us move forward with confidence and trust. However, this grace is most respectful of our freedom. Our saint beautifully descibes the interplay of grace and freedom: "Our free will is in no [way] forced or necessitated by grace . . . Grace is so gracious, and so graciously does it seize our hearts in order to draw them on, that it in no [way] impairs the liberty of our will. So powerful yet so delicately does it touch the spring of our spirit that our free will suffers no violence from it. Grace has the power not to overpower but to entice our heart. It has a holy violence, not to violate our liberty but to make it full of love. It acts strongly, yet so sweetly that our will is not crushed beneath so powerful an action. It presses but it does not oppress our freedom. The result is that under the very action of its power we can consent to its movement or resist as we please" (*TLG*, I:133).[2]

With such inspiring words, we can begin our journey full of hope, courage, confidence and love. To strengthen our resolve we pray with St. Francis de Sales:

> May it please you, O my God, eternal, almighty, and all-good, Father, Son and Holy Spirit, to confirm me in this resolution and to accept in the odor of sweetness this inward sacrifice of my heart. And as it has pleased you to grant me the will and the inspiration to do this, so also grant me the strength and the grace needed to perform it. O my God, you are my God, the God of my soul, and the God of my spirit. As such I acknowledge and adore you now and forever more. Live Jesus!" (*IDL*, pt. I, ch. 20).

---

2. *Treatise on the Love of God,* trans. with intro. J. K. Ryan (Stella Niagra, NY: De Sales Resource Center, 2007). Hereafter, TLG.

3. *Introduction to a Devout Life,* trans. with intro. J. K. Ryan (New York: Doubleday, 1966). Hereafter, IDL.

ST. FRANCIS DE SALES: A SHORT BIOGRAPHY

"There is no more difference between the written Gospel and the life of the saints than between the sheet music and the music sung" (*OEA*, 12:306).

INTRODUCTION

For Francis de Sales, the life of the saints is the Gospel lived with great vitality, enthusiasm, joy and love amid the most banal, trivial and ordinary events of daily life. Coming from all walks of life, saints are people who have fallen head over heels in love with God and deeply desire to proclaim and share that love with the whole world. Their lives are songs of continual praise and thanksgiving to God. Their great desire is that we join them in making this heavenly music on earth. We will find this to be especially true of the life of Francis de Sales who is widely known and honored for having reminded the people of his day and of ours that all of us are called to be saints. This is our destiny and our destination.

But as enamored as Francis was with the lives of the saints, it was always with a critical eye because the lives of certain saints were so extraordinary, outlandish and even bizarre. This led him to warn us that some saints are to be admired rather than imitated because of the extraordinary calling they have received from God. We will find that Francis de Sales is one of those saints that we will be most eager to imitate and love because of how well he understands the yearnings of the human heart and exhibited this in his writings and in his life. This is what particularly "grabs" us about this saint.

CHILDHOOD

Nature, nurture and grace conspired to shape Francis's life in many charming and attractive ways. Although he spoke and wrote French and helped to develop the modern French language, he was not French but a native of the Duchy of Savoy. In his day, this duchy covered areas that are now part of France, Switzerland and Italy. He was born in the Chateau De Sales in Thorens, Savoy in 1567. This period was rife with political and religious strife that was literally tearing apart not only countries and fiefdoms, but also many families because of deep-seated religious animosity and hatred. It was a time when the Church was in dire need of internal reform and externally assaulted by doctrinal onslaughts from Protestant reformers.

EDUCATION

Francis's father, M. de Boisy, a very respected member of the nobility, wanted to assure that his firstborn had the proper upbringing to assume his responsibilities as a nobleman and as the eventual head of the family. His early education took place in the nearby towns of La Roche and Annecy. From there, he went on to study the liberal arts at the Jesuit Collège de Clermont in Paris. In addition, to his liberal arts studies, he learned horsemanship, how to fence and how to dance—

activities that were part of a nobleman's upbringing.

All was not smooth sailing during his student days in Paris. He suffered from severe depression when he was about 18- or 19- years-old that cast a long and distressing shadow over his student life for about six weeks and almost led him to despair of his salvation. At that time, theological circles were all abuzz about the nature of predestination, greatly influenced by the teachings of Luther and Calvin. He could not shake off the idea that he was destined to perdition no matter what he did.

One day, when he was particularly overwhelmed by the feeling of despair, he slipped into one of the churches of the Latin Quarter. He knelt down before the statue of Our Lady of Deliverance, and made a very moving prayer of complete abandonment to God's will saying, "I will love you always, O Lord, at least in this life! At least in this life will I love you, if it is not given me to love you in eternity" (Lajeunie, I:71). Then he recited the *Memorare* and was immediately overcome with peace and serenity. The nature and cause of this temptation, trial or struggle are disputed by the saint's biographers. It was apparently due to the tension between the flesh and the spirit. We will see below where this trial profoundly marked his spirituality with optimism and joy.

To fully understand the nature of his struggle, it is helpful to mention another influence on his life at that time. In addition to pursuing a liberal arts education at Clermont, his mentor permitted him to study theology as well. He was fortunate to attend the lectures on the Song of Songs, or Canticle of Canticles, given by the renowned Benedictine teacher of Hebrew and scripture scholar, Gilbert Génébrard, to whom he later pays tribute in his *Treatise on the Love of God,* which is considered to be a lengthy commentary on the Canticle. Génébrard's approach to the Canticle opened up new horizons for the young student and made him appreciate God's relation with humanity as one great and glorious love story. This little book of scripture along with his personal experience as spiritual director to a number of women, principally St. Jane de Chantal, gave him profound insights into the feminine side of spirituality. This experience brought a good deal of balance to his own spirituality, which has been aptly characterized by the British Salesian scholar, Elisabeth Stopp, as "inspired common sense."

After completing his studies in Paris, he returned for a brief stay in Savoy. His father had ambitious plans for him as a lawyer. So he went on to study law for his father's sake and theology for his own sake at the University of Padua, which was reputedly one of the finest universities of its day. If the emotional and psychological struggle subsided in Paris, the intellectual struggle with the problem of predestination, the desire for a deeper understanding of this experience, was renewed at the University of Padua. For our saint it was essential to resolve this problem because it involved one's image of God, the nature of human freedom, and the value of human life. In his reflections, he focused on the scriptural passages that stressed God's infinite mercy and his desire that all should be saved. He concluded that the first blessing God gives us is to predestine us to the Church, which he called a convocation. In other words, the saint viewed God primarily as predestining us to live a life "with and for others"[4] in the Church, which he called the "assembly of love." Moreover, these reflections left him with a firm and unassailable conviction that God's providence provides us with all the means necessary to achieve this common vocation, this common calling, namely, to live in communion with God and with one another.

While at Padua, he intensified his seriousness of living a deeply spiritual life by writing a series of spiritual exercises and rules for guiding his interpersonal relations, known as the "Rules of Padua," and taking as a spiritual advisor, Antonio Possevino, a Jesuit who was exceptionally learned and prudent. It was here that we begin to see how he laid the foundations for the devout life, which he further fleshed out in his numerous letters of spiritual direction and in his two spiritual classics—*Introduction to The Devout Life* and the *Treatise on the Love of God*. He brilliantly completed his studies and obtained a doctorate in both canon and civil law.

---

1. E. Schillebeeckx, O.P., *God and Man* (New York: Sheed and Ward, 1969), 110.

VOCATION

With his eldest son equipped with one of the best educations of his time and blessed with so many appealing social graces, it is no wonder that M. de Boisy had big plans for his son to enter the law profession. However, Francis felt himself strongly called to the priesthood. This, of course, dashed the high hopes of his father, who finally consented for him to follow his priestly calling. Francis was ordained to the priesthood in 1593 and made provost of the cathedral chapter of Geneva. However, he had to exercise this office in the little town of Annecy since the bishop of Geneva, was exiled from his see city which was occupied at that time by the Calvinists. His initial address as provost to the members of the cathedral chapter, which aggressively wanted to take back its cathedral in Geneva, set an unaccustomed irenic and peaceful tone. He declared that, "We shall bring down the walls of Geneva with *charity*; we must invade Geneva with *charity*; we must recover Geneva with *charity*" (Ravier, 57). He reminded them that one of the primary reasons for the loss of the Catholic faith and the success of Calvinism was the infidelity and ignorance of the clergy.

Francis realized that there can be no true reform unless one reforms himself. So he threw himself into his priestly work with great zeal and fervor. He heard confessions, catechized and preached with great intensity and effectiveness, visited the poor, the sick and those in prison. He fulfilled all of his responsibilities with great dedication and love.

MISSION

Aware of the great risks, Francis's bishops asked for volunteers to reclaim the Calvinists in the Chablais region of the duchy for the Catholic faith rather than to assign anyone to this perilous and demanding apostolate. Francis offered his services, which were eagerly accepted by the bishop. He and his cousin, Louis de Sales, began this missionary work in the fall of 1594. Because of the hostility of the Calvinist ministers and a number of their adherents as well as political obstacles, the mission proved to be much more challenging and dangerous than Francis originally anticipated. His strategy was to begin a respectful dialogue with the Calvinists on doctrinal differences. Much to his chagrin, hardly anyone showed up when he preached because of the misconceptions they had about Catholic priests and the pressure that was put on them by their leaders. To overcome this, he wrote leaflets on various topics explaining the Catholic teaching, posted them in public places and placed them under the doorways. This endeavor later earned him the title of "Patron of Journalists." These writings eventually were published as the *Controversies*, and serve even today as a solid source explaining Catholic teaching. Despite the many hardships Francis had to endure daily, his missionary zeal reaped significant fruit and brought several thousands back to the Catholic faith.

In 1602, Bishop de Granier sent him to Paris on a diplomatic and religious mission. During his extended stay there, he achieved great renown as a preacher and spiritual advisor and was eagerly sought after by many. He frequented almost daily the circle of Mme. Acarie where he came in contact with the foremost spiritual leaders of France of the day who represented several rich and important currents of Catholic spirituality. This experience greatly helped him to refine his own spirituality, deeply influenced by St. Teresa of Ávila. On his return to Annecy, Francis was consecrated bishop of Geneva on December 8, 1602.

Francis was much in demand as a preacher and was invited to give the series of Lenten sermons in several dioceses of France. On one of these occasions in 1604, he encountered Jane de Chantal, who eventually asked him to be her spiritual director. This encounter would prove to be extremely auspicious not only for Jane herself, but for the Church in France and for the deepening and spreading of Salesian spirituality. As a recent widow with four children and a host of responsibilities, Jane deeply longed to become a saint. Francis's whole strategy in guiding her was to free her to love. The overall principle he gave her was, "Do all through love and nothing through constraint." He stressed the intimate connection that exists between love and freedom and strove to inculcate in her a spirit of freedom. This consisted essentially in a complete detachment of one's will in order to follow the known will of God. This relationship with Jane, as Francis readily and gratefully admitted, was mutually enriching and rewarding. It became one of the most renowned examples of a spiritual friendship.

The writing and publication of his *Introduction to the Devout Life* in 1609 was an outgrowth of his extensive experience as a spiritual director. This great, spiritual classic has withstood the test of four centuries because of its down-to-earth approach to holiness. Its basic purpose is to demonstrate in a clear, convincing and attractive manner that holiness is not the exclusive domain of the clergy or religious, but that everyone is called to holiness no matter what his or her station in life. This book is a practical manual on how to achieve devotion, that is, holiness in our everyday, mundane activities. Francis achieves this by teaching us how to pray, how to choose and practice the virtues suitable to our state in life, how to develop spiritual friendships, how to deal with temptations and how to persevere in our choice of pursuing holiness. In a word, he shows us how to "Live Jesus!" enthusiastically and joyfully.

As noted above, Francis's encounter with Jane was to have significant consequences for the Church. With Jane de Chantal he founded the Congregation of the Visitation of Holy Mary in 1610. Unlike most of the religious institutes of that day, the Visitation accepted women of weak physical constitution who could not or who did not desire to practice the demanding physical austerities of the other women's orders. Francis considered the spirit of the Visitation to be "a spirit of deepest humility toward God and gentleness toward neighbor. Because where there is less bodily austerity, there must be the greatest gentleness of heart" *(Spiritual Conferences, 97)*. The order grew very rapidly and played an important role in the reform of the Church.

Francis was keenly aware of how essential our human relationships are for our growth in the spiritual life. He not only gave a great deal to the Visitandines in his many spiritual conferences, but also received in return great insights from them. He gives credit in his Preface to the *Treatise on Love of God,* of the great debt he owed to them, especially to St. Jane. Without the Visitation, this book, which is intended for those who want to delve deeper into the devout life, would probably never have been written. Although it is challenging to read, it remains one of the most penetrating and illuminating works on the nature of divine love and its relationship to human love.

The pastoral concerns of Francis's vast diocese, which covered many small hamlets in mountainous areas, as well as the reform of his clergy, and the growth and needs of the Visitation, made great demands on his time. Despite these exacting and exhausting demands, he was still able to give spiritual guidance, mainly through correspondence, to a number of people who sought his counsel. His extant correspondence fills eleven volumes. Francis died in 1622 from a painful illness in the humble gardener's cottage attached to the Visitation monastery of Lyons, France.

During his lifetime, he was highly regarded as a saint and much beloved by people in all ranks of life. He was canonized in 1665 by Pope Alexander VII and declared a Doctor of the Church in 1877 by Pope Pius IX. Francis had a remarkable gift for showing us how to connect our head with our heart. His fascinating and engaging view of the human person lies at the basis of his teaching and spirit. "Man is the perfection of the universe; the mind is the perfection of man. Love is the perfection of the mind, and charity is the perfection of love" (*TLG*, II:141).

IMPORTANT DATES
IN THE LIFE OF
ST. FRANCIS DE SALES

1567   Born in the Chateau de Sales, Thorens, Savoy

1580–88   Pursues a liberal education at the Jesuit Collège de Clermont, Paris

1588–90   Studies law and theology at the University of Padua and receives a doctorate in both canon and civil law in 1591

1593   Appointed Provost of the cathedral chapter of Geneva and ordained to the priesthood in Annecy

1594–98   Missionary work in the Chablais region

1602   Consecrated Bishop of Geneva

1604   Encounters Jane de Chantal in Dijon

1609   Publishes the *Introduction to the Devout Life*

1610   Co-founds with Jane de Chantal the Visitation of Holy Mary

1616   Publishes *Treatise on the Love of God*

1622   Dies at Lyons, December 28

1665   Canonized a saint by Pope Alexander VII

1877   Declared a Doctor of the Universal Church by Pope Pius IX

1923   Made Patron Saint of Journalists by Pope Pius XI

THE OBLATES OF ST. FRANCIS DE SALES: A BRIEF HISTORY

FOUNDATION

The attractiveness and effectiveness of the life and teaching of St. Francis de Sales (1567–1622) had a great deal of appeal even in the saint's lifetime. The order of the Visitation of Holy Mary co-founded by the saint and his very close friend and collaborator, St. Jane de Chantal (1572–1641), did much in a very short time to help reform religious life as well as the Church by living and promoting the teachings and spirit of the saint. Encouraged by St. Jane, Francis planned to found an institute of priests that would be formed in the same spirit as the Visitation. However, since he had so much on his plate, he was not able to realize this plan. A few years after the saint's death in 1622, Fr. Raymond Bonal (1600–1653), a priest of the diocese of Rodez, did establish, with the support of St. Jane, the Priests of St. Mary, known as the Bonalists, who had as their aim and purpose to exemplify the teaching and spirit of St. Francis de Sales. For various reasons, this congregation did not survive for long after the death of its founder.

About two centuries later, the idea was revived by a Visitation sister and Superior of the monastery in Troyes, France, Mother Mary de Sales Chappuis (1793–1875). She kept after the monastery's chaplain, Fr. Louis Brisson (1817–1908), to found a congregation of priests that would revive the vision and plans of St. Francis de Sales and St. Jane de Chantal. However, he was very disinclined to listen to her because not only did he not see how he could obtain the material resources as well as the vocations, but also because the suggestion came, as he later frankly admitted, from a woman, whom, nonetheless he greatly admired. In fact, he became so frustrated with her as she became more insistent that he was the one destined by God to found this congregation, that he said in exasperation, "Who will deliver me from this woman?" So Fr. Brisson asked for some sign from God and did receive a vision of the Lord who appeared to him in one of the parlors of the monastery as he was waiting to speak to Mother Mary de Sales. He did not reveal this vision for almost three decades. So over a thirty-year period or more, he turned a deaf ear to her.

Fr. Brisson was urged to found this congregation not only by Mother de Sales Chappuis, but also by Bishop Mermillod (1824–1892) of the diocese of Lauzanne-Geneva. The occasion presented itself when his own bishop asked him to take over the administration of the only Catholic secondary school in the diocese. In 1888, he was able to gather several priests interested in teaching at the school. This group began to live a common life with the approval of Bishop Ravinet (1801–1881). In 1875, the Congregation with the name of the Oblates of St. Francis de Sales (also known as the De Sales Oblates) received initial approval of Pope Pius IX by the decree of praise *(decretum laudis)*. The following year, five members made their first profession of vows to Bishop Cortet (1817-1898), who succeeded the ailing Bishop Ravinet. Pope Leo XIII gave official approval of the Constitutions in 1887.

CHARISM

The charism of the Oblates was greatly influenced by Mother Mary de Sales Chappuis, who was considered to be the foremost interpreter of the teachings of St. Francis de Sales. Even though Fr. Brisson for years resisted her suggestion to found the Oblates. Over a forty-year period of being chaplain to the Troyes Visitation, he gratefully admitted that his understanding of the teaching and spirit of St. Francis de Sales was shaped primarily and profoundly by the Good Mother, as she was so lovingly referred to. Her vision of an Oblate was to see, as she expressed, "Jesus Christ walking again on earth." This was certainly a tall order and one not easily or readily achieved. However, the way it was to be achieved in her view was by the faithful practice of a little book known as the *Spiritual Directory*. This is not, as one might suppose, a list of spiritual matters or of various spiritualities, but rather, as one early Oblate explained: "It is a very small book composed by St. Francis de Sales, both for himself and for the souls whom he guided. It is intended to give us for each occupation the proper interior spiritual dispositions, and to lead us gradually by means of oft-repeated communication with God to a habitual intimate union with God, which more and more instills into the faithful soul the Divine" (Fr. John Isenring, *The Echo of the Oblates of St. Francis de Sales,* vol. 1, no. 1 [Sept. 1906]:43).

This *Directory*, initially composed by St. Francis de Sales, was later revised by St. Jane and further revised by Fr. Brisson to make it applicable to the Oblate life. It encapsulates the teaching and spirit of the saint, who, both the Good Mother and Fr. Brisson firmly believed, was sanctified by its faithful practice. Although it encapsulates Salesian teaching, it opens one to a study, love, appropriation and spreading of the saint's spirit and teachings. For Fr. Brisson the faithful practice of the *Spiritual Directory* is the essential identifying characteristic of a De Sales Oblate because it is his privileged way of union with Jesus and with his neighbor, especially the explicit practice of the Direction of Intention in small and great actions throughout each day. In this way, the Oblate engraves on his heart the saint's motto and the Oblate motto, "Live Jesus." Once we have Jesus in our heart, then St. Francis de Sales says we will have him in all of our actions. The *Spiritual Directory* is intended to help the De Sales Oblate learn how to be gentle and humble of heart.

MISSION

Although the initial apostolate of the Oblates of St. Francis de Sales was the education of youth, it had a much broader mission, one that Fr. Brisson described as "entering the world such as it is." During its first few years, the De Sales Oblates were in great demand as educators. From 1869 to 1889, Fr. Brisson founded five schools in various French cities, no easy task when one considers the hostility of the government to religious orders and especially to their schools. The DeSales Oblates were called upon by the Society of the Faith in 1882 to establish a mission in Pella, South Africa. This was soon followed several years later by missions in South America (Brazil, Uruguay and Ecuador) and foundations in England, Greece, the United States, Austria and Germany.

This rapid expansion abroad was due in large part to the anticlerical and anti-Catholic policies and laws of the French government, which began to delegitimize, confiscate and auction off properties of various religious orders. This unjust action affirmed the well-known saying: "When God closes a window, he opens a door." And Fr. Brisson saw many doors opening before him, many more than he could send his De Sales Oblates through. To pay tribute a few days after his death to Fr. Brisson's accomplishment, a newspaper ran an article in the form of an imaginary dialogue entitled "The Two Brisson Cousins." It highlighted the odd kinship between Fr. Brisson and his cousin, François Brisson, President of the Chamber of Deputies. The latter boasted of how the "block," a syndicate of the Free-Masons, who, at every opportunity took hostile actions against the Catholic Church, had elevated him to his present position and to whom he owed everything. He saw in this help and support what it meant "to love the Republic." In his riposte, Fr. Brisson is quoted as saying:

Cousin, I have loved my country above all, and that's why I founded congregations of men and women who have made France loved as far as Brazil, Ecuador, the Antilles, Central Africa, and South America, England, the United States, Austria—all have opened their doors to my Oblates. You, however, have persecuted and exiled them . . . In France, as elsewhere—everywhere—my religious men and women have consecrated their lives to the education of children; they have welcomed and fed orphans; they have founded shelters for workers, and established institutions for the preservation and care of people. And you have dared to strike them! (*Petit Patriote*, 1905).

PRESENT STATUS

Today Oblates are located in nine countries: Austria, Brazil, France Germany, Holland, Italy, Switzerland, and Uruguay with missions in seven countries: Benin, Ecuador, Haiti, India, Namibia, Mexico, and South Africa. Missions in India and Haiti are witnessing a significant increase in Oblate vocations while the numbers in the European countries and the United States are sadly declining. Over the years, the major apostolates for the American Oblates have been the education of youth and parish work. Despite declining numbers, the two American Provinces have been branching out to realize Fr. Brisson's mission of "entering the world as it is" by placing a major emphasis on apostolates that serve the disadvantaged and the poor. This is particularly demonstrated by the De Sales Service Works (DSW), which networks with a number of social service agencies in Camden, New Jersey by providing volunteers schooled in Salesian spirituality and retreats in an inner city setting that sensitize the retreatants, usually high school and college students, to the needs of the underprivileged. The DeSales Oblates have also founded a Nativity School, which provides tuition-free education in grades 5 through 8 to inner city underprivileged boys to prepare them to enroll tuition-free in academically challenging private secondary schools.

Since Vatican II, the Oblates, like many other religious orders, have become more aware of their raison d'être and have looked more carefully at their individual inspiration. The specific charism of the Oblates as noted above is to live and promote the spirit and teachings of St. Francis de Sales as understood by their founder, Fr. Brisson and their inspirer, Mother Mary de Sales Chappuis. In one of the Chapters of renewal, the Oblates established over thirty years ago an International Commission on Salesian Studies (ICSS), which has the specific mission of promoting Salesian studies worldwide. These studies include those "relative to St. Francis de Sales, St. Jane de Chantal, Father Brisson, Mother Mary de Sales Chappuis, the Sisters of the Visitation of Holy Mary, the Oblates of St. Francis de Sales, the Oblate Sisters of St. Francis de Sales, the De Sales Secular Institute and the entire Salesian family." It does this primarily through a biennial newsletter published in five languages (English, French, German, Italian, Brazilian Portuguese, and Spanish). By means of a Web site available at http://www4.desales.edu/~salesian/resources.html, it publishes and archives these newsletters as well as provides various resources on Salesian spirituality and links to all the other Oblate provinces and regions and related websites. In addition, it provides grants to Oblates for various projects, programs and translations to fulfill its objective.

Several Provinces have allotted considerable resources to promote the Oblate-Salesian charism. Of note are the De Sales Resources and Ministries Center of the Toledo-Detroit Province, the De Sales Spirituality Center of the Wilmington-Philadelphia Province, the Salesian Center for Faith and Culture at De Sales University, founded and administered by the Oblates, and the Franz von Sales Verlag (Francis de Sales Publishing House) of the German-Speaking Province, which, among other things has been publishing the Annual Yearbook of Salesian Studies (*Jahrbuch für Salesianische Studien*) for almost forty years. All of these endeavors have proven to be very successful and responsive to a worldwide interest in Salesian spirituality.

ST. FRANCIS DE SALES
AND THE
LENTEN SEASON

One of the best ways to link St. Francis de Sales to the season of Lent is by his preaching. The state of preaching in the Catholic church of his day was, for the most part, abysmal. Here is where the criticisms leveled against the Catholic Church by the Reformers, who placed great value on preaching, hit home with our saint. He worked mightily to renew preaching in the Church and is considered to have made a considerable impact in its renewal, especially by his own preaching and his little treatise on preaching addressed to the brother of St. Jane de Chantal, Archbishop André Fremyot.[5]

In this treatise, he advises the young prelate to eschew the then prevalent method of preaching, which emphasized a grandiloquence that was intended to promote the preacher rather than to proclaim the

---

5. See *On the Preacher and Preaching: A Letter by Francis de Sales,* trans. with intro. and notes John K. Ryan (Chicago: Henry Regnery, 1964).

Good News. He believed that the primary aim of the preacher was to speak to the heart of his listeners in a simple, direct and unaffected manner. "Our words must be set aflame," our saint asserts, "not by shouts and unrestrained gestures, but by inward affection. They must issue from the heart rather than from our mouth. We must speak well, but heart speaks to heart, and the tongue only to peoples ears" (*Lenten Sermons,* xx).

Furthermore, he taught that preaching was the ordinary way that God sends us his inspirations. For him, inspirations play an indispensable role in our sanctification. This was certainly an extremely optimistic view of preaching in view of its lamentable state. It explains, however, why he never passed up an opportunity to preach. In fact, his own father criticized him for preaching too often: "Provost, you preach too often; I hear the bell ring even on week days . . . Now you have made preaching so common . . . and no one will think very much of you" (*Lenten Sermons,* xvii-xviii). In spite of his father's criticism, our saint took his responsibility to preach as a bishop very seriously as required by this office and emphasized by the Council of Trent.

In St. Francis de Sales's day, the Lenten season was celebrated with a great deal of solemnity. It was customary for a bishop or a nobleman to invite a bishop from another diocese, to preach a series of sermons to the people of the diocese or area. Our saint was greatly admired and sought after as an excellent preacher. During his episcopacy, he accepted twenty of these invitations. It was while preaching a Lenten series in Dijon that he fortuitously encountered St. Jane de Chantal. Fortunately, a number of his Lenten sermons have come down to us, and I have drawn from them numerous excerpts as reflections on the Lenten Gospel readings.

It is important to remember that very few people in our saint's day could read and write and that the spoken word was paramount in communicating with others. This is why preaching played such an indispensable role in teaching and in encouraging the faithful. This was the primary source of knowledge of their faith. Our saint realized this and made extraordinary efforts to have the people gain a deeper knowledge of the scriptures and of Jesus, perhaps having in the back of his mind the saying of St. Jerome that "Ignorance of Scripture is ignorance of Christ." His primary purpose in preaching, especially in his Lenten sermons, was to give his listeners knowledge of the crucified Jesus. He effectively described Jesus' sufferings so that they could come to appreciate the depth of his love for us. We learn how to love at the foot of the Cross: "It is at the foot of this Cross that we should remain always. It is the place where the imitators of our Sovereign Master and Savior ordinarily abide. For it is from the Cross that they receive the heavenly liqueur of holy charity. It streams out in great profusion from a divine source, the bosom of our good God's divine mercy. He loves us with a love so firm, so solid, so ardent and so persevering that death itself could not cool it in the least. Quite the contrary, it warmed and increased it infinitely" (*Lenten Sermons*, 97).

Contemplating the sacred wounds of Jesus also makes us also aware of Jesus' love for us, especially his wounded side that opens his heart to us: "What will we do, dear souls, what will become, I ask you, when through the sacred wound of his side we perceive that most adorable heart of our Master, aflame with love for us—that heart where we will see each of our names written in letters of love! 'Is it possible, O my dear Savior,' we will say, 'that you have loved me so much that you have engraved my name in your heart?'. . . Jesus, enlarging on these words [of Is 49:15–16], will say: 'Even if it were possible for a woman to forget her child, yet I will never forget you, since I bear your name engraved in My Heart'" (*Lenten Sermons,* 62). The same idea is conveyed when he speaks of Jesus' wounds: "These wounds are an everlasting monument to his love, but of a most tender and generous love. O lovable wounds of my Savior! O wounds that only emanate love! 'O most lovable wounds of our Lord Jesus Christ!'"(*OEA,* 8:429).

Lent was for our saint not only a time to get closer to God, but also to get closer to one another. A vertical spirituality must also result in a horizontal one that brings us closer to our neighbor since this is what Jesus set out to accomplish by his suffering and death; it must bring about a holy communion among ourselves. The power to accomplish this comes from Jesus' Passion. "He poured out his blood on the earth even to the last drop, as if to make a sacred mortar [Col 1:20] with which he would mortar, unite, join and attach to each other all the stones of his Church, that is, the faithful . . . We have all alike been washed with this precious blood, as with a sacred mortar, to bind and unite our hearts together!" (*Lenten Sermons,* 95).

Being united in love with others brings about the true portrait of God among us: "No one is to excuse himself from this and say that he does not know that he is to love his neighbor as himself, because God has imprinted this truth in the bottom of our hearts in creating all of us in the image and likeness of each other. Bearing the image of God in ourselves, all of us are consequently the image of each other. Together we constitute the image of one portrait, that of God" (*Lenten Sermons,* 88).

The season of Lent for our saint is an especially graced time to shape our own cross as to conform to that of Jesus: "[Our Divine Master] . . . spent His entire life even shaping his cross, suffering a thousand persecutions from the very ones to whom he was doing so much good and for whom he laid down his life . . . We must do the same . . . ; we too should shape our cross in suffering for one another as the Savior taught us; in giving our life for those very ones who would take it from us, as he so lovingly did; in spending ourselves for our neighbor, not only in agreeable things, but also in those which are painful and disagreeable such as bearing lovingly these persecutions which might in some fashion cool our heart towards our brothers"(*Lenten Sermon,* 93). By shaping our own cross, we find the strength and the courage to be human, as human as Jesus was: "In becoming man, he has taken our likeness and given us his. Oh how earnestly should we summon up our courage to live according to what we are and to imitate as perfectly as possible him who came into this world to teach us what we need to do to preserve in ourselves this beauty and divine resemblance which He has so completely repaired and embellished in us!" (*Lenten Sermons,* 91).

Our saint in his Lenten sermons knows how to make Jesus come alive for us in ways that deeply touch our hearts and transform our lives.

He holds up to us Jesus' virtues in his suffering and death as examples for us to imitate so that his life may dwell in us more vigorously and more vibrantly. The two virtues which best exemplify Our Lord are those he himself urges to learn from him, namely, humility and gentleness. He brings this out in a sermon on Palm Sunday describing why Jesus decided to enter Jerusalem riding on a humble beast of burden.

By accepting the numerous invitations to preach a Lenten series of sermons in other dioceses and of energetically and enthusiastically assuming this task in his own diocese, St. Francis de Sales made many Lenten journeys with the faithful and helped them to understand and appreciate that "[Jesus] willed . . . to make himself companion of our miseries so afterwards to make us companions of his glory" (*TLG*, I:113).

During this journey, we freely and lovingly join the company of the Lord Jesus and Francis de Sales. This will give us numerous opportunities as we travel with them to speak to them openly and frankly of our concerns, our fears, our hopes and our desires and to see how these are aligned with or need to be realigned with what the Father expects of us. This realignment will call for a great deal of discipline and of self-giving love that may at times be challenging and even crucifying.

These intimate conversations constitute for our saint the essence of prayer in which we speak to God and God speaks to us. The difficult part is listening to what God has to say to us. As Arthur Conan Doyle reminds us: "We have but one mouth and two ears to indicate that there is twice as much work for the one as for the other"(see *White Company*). In close company with Jesus, we try to learn from him how he prayed and was always conscious of doing whatever the Father asked of him. This is why our saint loved to dwell on the Lord's Prayer and its implications for our prayer life. In fact, he saw this prayer as the most perfect prayer since it was given to us by Jesus himself. He urges us to take one petition each day as a springboard for spiritual aspirations, about which will speak more later.

The Lenten season affords us the grace-filled opportunity of deepening our prayer life so that we can more readily, faithfully and perseveringly "Live Jesus!," the motto our saint wishes to engrave on our hearts. It is through various forms of prayer that we access the heart of Jesus and our own heart, the core and center of our being. Once we have Jesus in our heart, then we will have him in all of our actions since the heart is the wellspring that gives value and meaning to all of our actions both interior and exterior. All the mortifications and acts of self-denial that we practice are undertaken not so much to achieve self-mastery or self-discipline but rather to open us up more to God's love. It is by means of this love that we will be able to travel the way of the cross and experience firsthand the Lord's sufferings, death and resurrection. It is meant to be a Passover experience for us where we pass over from death to self to a new and reinvigorated life in Jesus. This can only be accomplished through love as the first letter of John informs us: "We know that we have passed [passed over] from death to life because we love our brothers [and sisters]. Whoever does not love remains in death." (1 Jn 3:14). So the purpose and goal of this Lenten journey is a genuine resurrection or Passover experience that will deepen our spiritual life and radically change it.

The rallying cry for the holy season of Lent is "prayer, almsgiving and fasting." For our saint the latter two—almsgiving and fasting—are forms of prayer since they carry out in external actions the subject of our prayer. They should be the result of our prayer, which is not merely conversing with God, but to be effective must have a palpable and salutary effect on our lives and the lives of others. Fasting can help reign in our errant impulses and selfish inclinations and help us focus on the things that really matter. Almsgiving leads us to share the good things we possess with others and deepens our desire to give of ourselves to God and to one another.

ST. FRANCIS
DE SALES
ON PRAYER

In prayer, we do "not want the blessings of God, but the God of blessings" (*TLG*, II:22).

INTRODUCTION TO SALESIAN PRAYER

For St. Francis de Sales there can be no genuine spiritual life without prayer because prayer is what connects us to God and through God's grace gives us an ever deepening understanding of ourselves so that we may readily connect with others. He explains the need and the efficacy of prayer in this way: "Since prayer places our intellect in the brilliance of God's light and exposes our will to the warmth of heavenly love, nothing else so effectively purifies our intellect of ignorance and our will of depraved affections. It is a stream of holy water that flows forth and makes the plants of our good desires grow green and flourish and quenches the passions within our hearts" (*IDL*, pt. 2, ch.1). Prayer also quenches our thirst for God and paradoxically makes us even thirstier for God and his love. This thirst is what urges us to continue to pray and not lose heart.

The kind of prayer he strongly recommends is what he calls "mental prayer" or the "prayer of the heart." It is called mental because we propose to our minds various considerations, especially those centering on the Passion and death of Our Lord. It is called the prayer of the heart because these considerations are intended to result in affections that move our heart to make concrete resolutions that are to be carried out daily. In this way, our prayer does not remain sterile but issues in actions that lead us to express our love for God, especially as demonstrated by our love for others. He sets forth a method for mental prayer or meditation to help those who are novices in prayer and need some structure to make their prayer productive. Of course, St. Francis de Sales is no slave to method in prayer; he realizes that the most important principle in prayer is to follow the promptings of the Holy Spirit.

PREPARATION OF THE DAY

Our day is to begin with prayer. As we awaken, our saint proposes that we think of this action as an image of our resurrection and repeat the words of Job: "I know that my Redeemer lives, and that on the last day I will rise again. My God, grant that this be to eternal glory; this hope rests in my inmost being." Morning prayer begins as soon as we get up by adoring God and thanking him for having kept us from sin during the night. It is to be done rather quickly while we are getting dressed and washed. He reminds us that each particular day has been given to us by God so as to love him more deeply. To do this, we must prepare our day by foreseeing the various actions, duties and activities we will be engaged in and noting in particular any occasion that is liable to cause difficulty of one kind or another. When we anticipate some problem, we ask the Lord to give us the grace and the proper disposition for facing it. For example, if we foresee that we have to deal with some disagreeable person with whom we are inclined to lose our patience, then we discuss this briefly with the Lord and ask him to give us the humility and gentleness we need in order not to unnecessarily upset this person. Here we can remind ourselves of the words of Jesus who urges us to learn from him these two essential virtues when he says, "Learn of me for I am gentle and humble of heart" (Mt 11:29).

MEDITATION

The prayer of the Preparation of the Day is intended to prepare us for the prayer of meditation, mental prayer or the "prayer of the heart." Since this may be difficult for those unfamiliar with it, he sets forth a short method in *Introduction to the Devout Life* (pt. 2) to assist beginners. The four major parts of his method of meditating are (1) Preparation, (2) Considerations, (3) Affections and Resolutions, and (4) Conclusion and Spiritual Bouquet. Let us briefly consider each one of these.

In the preparation, we make ourselves aware of God's presence by considering that God is everywhere or that he is particularly present in our hearts, or that Jesus is looking down on us or is right beside us as we pray. Making ourselves conscious of God's presence is extremely important not only for mental prayer but for all kinds of prayer. Our saint gives two reasons for this, namely, one to give God the honor and praise that is his due and the other to make us well disposed to hear God speak to us in his revealed word, his inspirations and "the inner stirrings of our heart." Second, we then call upon God's grace to make a good meditation, realizing as Scripture tells us that we do not know how to pray. The third part of the preparation is the selection of the subject on which we propose to our imagination and mind to dwell on. The privileged subject for St. Francis de Sales is the Passion and death of Our Lord, utilizing primarily for this purpose the various scriptural narratives. For our saint, there is nothing that can more convince us of his unfathomable love for us and inflame our hearts to receive and to reciprocate this love. For the Lenten season, prayerful readings of the daily scriptural passages, especially the gospels, the night before can serve as an excellent preparation for our daily meditation.

Next comes the considerations. Here we turn over in our minds the various aspects of the Christian mystery we have selected. We do this not in the manner of study in order to become more learned but rather to move our hearts and wills so that we become more loving. Here is where the imagination can be helpful in aiding us to picture in our minds a particular event in the life of Our Lord, conversing with him or with others who are involved in this mystery. In this part of the meditation properly so called, we place our minds "in the brilliance of God's light" in order to open up "our will to the warmth of his heavenly love."

The very heart of the Salesian method of meditation is found in the affections and resolutions. Its whole aim and purpose are to arouse our wills to make us more affectionate, compassionate and virtuous by formulating practical resolutions that we can carry out that very day. It was a firm conviction of our saint that we have been wounded more in our will than in our intellect. We very often know what we must do but lack the strength and the resolve to carry out what we know we ought to do. Meditation is intended to strengthen our will weakened by original sin and to assist us to customize or personalize the spiritual or devout life to fit our specific weaknesses, strengths and duties.

Finally, to help assure that the effects of our meditation will be carried over to our daily lives, we need to have a "wrap-up" of our meditation, which our saint calls the conclusion and spiritual bouquet. In this wrap-up, we thank God for the affections and resolutions we made and offer them up to him along with the life and sufferings of his only Son. We realize that without God's help, we will not be able to carry through on the resolutions we have made unless his grace is there to assist us. As a very perceptive psychologist, our saint recommends that we make a spiritual bouquet, that is, that we select a word or thought from our meditation that particularly struck us and can readily recall for us throughout the day the highlights of our meditation. He uses the image of a person who walks through a flower garden and as he leaves plucks one of the flowers to smell its fragrance, bringing back to mind the pleasant experience.

It is not necessary to practice meditation in a church or chapel. Some do their morning meditation in some quite spot in or around one's home or while traveling to and from work or even while jogging or doing one's fast paced walking in the morning.

This method of meditation is not intended to be rigid. If we experience affections before considerations, then we should dwell on them since the considerations are intended to arouse our affections and lead to concrete resolutions. The primary rule for all prayer is to follow the promptings of the Holy Spirit, who often speaks to our hearts and like a lover whispers words of love in the ear of his beloved. Our saint calls this the "secret of secrets" of prayer.

CONTEMPLATION

Our saint understands the relationship between meditation and contemplation as being based on our desire to be loving and to be loved. "Desire to obtain love causes us to meditate," he states, "but the love obtained causes us to contemplate." He further elucidates this connection by saying: "Meditation is the mother of love, but contemplation is its daughter." Ordinarily contemplation results from meditation. The latter takes effort and makes us look in detail at the subject of the mystery we are dwelling on. Whereas, contemplation gives us a sweeping view of the mystery without going into detail and is effortless. It is a special gift from God. In contemplation, we take great delight in God's love for us. Essentially it is what we will be doing in heaven for all eternity. "How happy are we to begin here below what we shall do forever in heaven! To it may God, Father, Son and Holy Spirit lead us. Amen" (see *TLG*, bk. 6). Our saint warns us that we may never experience contemplative prayer as he understands and explains it, but this should not upset us because it is not necessary for holiness. He assures us that there have been many who have led saintly lives without a contemplative prayer life.

SPIRITUAL RECOLLECTION
AND SPIRITUAL ASPIRATIONS

Since our saint intended to make holiness accessible to people in all walks of life, he realized that some people because of the many daily demands made on them cannot always set aside a half hour or more for meditation on a regular basis. For those who are loaded down with work, he recommends that frequently throughout the day they briefly retire within the chapels of their hearts. As we would expect, the special place for spiritual retirement that our saint recommends is found in the wounds of Our Lord, especially his wounded side. There we can feel the pulsating beat of Jesus' heart and experience the enormity of his love for us so that we may be more readily inclined to make our hearts beat in rhythm with his heart.

In one of his meditations, our saint proposes that we ask ourselves this question: "What did I think about, O my God, when I did not think of you? What did I remember when I forgot you? What did I love when I did not love you?"(*IDL*, pt. 1, ch. 10). These provocative questions are the basis for the practice of spiritual aspirations, which go hand in glove with spiritual recollection. These spiritual aspirations or ejaculatory prayers "are short, ardent movements of the heart" and may be expressed either in suitable words from scripture, especially the Psalms, or preferably in one's own words. To help us become proficient with this practice, St. Francis de Sales advises that: "A good way to accustom ourselves to making these ejaculations is to take the petitions of the Our Father one after another, choosing a sentence for each day" (*Sermons On Prayer*, 27). Furthermore, we are never too busy to practice them: "No one can be excused from making [this practice] because it can be made while coming and going about one's business . . . Who can prevent you from speaking to Him in the depth of your heart, since it makes no difference whether you speak to Him mentally or vocally?" (*Sermons on Prayer*, 26–27).

Our saint notes that when one falls in love with another person, he is constantly thinking about that other person and desiring to communicate his love and admiration. This same disposition is what should animate us in frequently thinking of God and expressing our love and longing for him, no matter how busy we are. Far from distracting us from our duties, it energizes us to fulfill them with greater love, purpose and dedication.

St. Francis de Sales privileges spiritual aspirations above all other forms of prayer because this form of prayer can replace them but cannot be replaced by any other kind of prayer. He expresses its importance in this way: "Without this exercise we cannot properly lead the contemplative life, and we can but poorly lead the active life. Without it rest is mere idleness, and labor is drudgery" (*IDL*, pt. 2, ch. 13).

PERSEVERANCE IN PRAYER

We must be attentive to the nature of prayer and to what we expect from prayer. In prayer, we focus on the God of consolations and not the consolations of God. There are times in our prayer when we no doubt feel consoled, supported and uplifted; we feel that God is present. However, when we experience difficulty in prayer and feel that God is not responding to our needs, we may be inclined to think that our prayer is not effective, that God is not listening, that God does not care. So we can easily become discouraged and weary of praying. On these occasions, our saint advises us: "Let us persevere in prayer all the time. For if Our Lord appears not to hear, it is not because he wants to reject us but because he wants us to cry out all the louder and make us experience the greatness of his mercy" (*OEA*, 10:229).

SCRIPTURE AND PRAYER

St. Cyprian succinctly expresses the essential relationship between Sacred Scripture and prayer when he says, "In Scripture, God speaks to us, and in prayer we speak to God." St. Francis de Sales would wholeheartedly subscribe to this saying and could not imagine the concept of prayer apart from scripture. He reveled in the medieval hermeneutics of the four senses or levels of biblical interpretation—the literal, allegorical, anagogical (moral) and tropological (eschatological)—but not uncritically, avoiding the excesses of the allegorical meaning. To utilize God's word profitably in prayer, we must first be familiar with its literal meaning. However, if we remain on this level, our prayer life would not draw upon all the richness that scripture provides. We must be open to the three other levels of meaning. Our saint stressed the spiritual and moral senses of Scripture in order to derive from them what we most need to be more closely united to God.

In understanding the nature of prayer, he was greatly influenced by the ideas of the Fathers of the Church and early spiritual writers. Like them, he sees prayer essentially as a conversation with God. In prayer, we listen very carefully to what God says to us, especially in his sacred word, and we in turn speak to him. It is a heart-to-heart conversation, a communication on the deepest level of our being where we pour out our hearts to God in order to be in communion with him and with all of those united to God. Here is where Sacred Scripture aids us greatly in prayer. For as St. Paul reminds us: "All Scripture inspired by God is useful for teaching and refutation for correction and for putting us in the way that is right with God, for communication and communion" (2 Tim 3:16, Basil Pennington's translation). It is a fundamental conviction of our saint that we are all capable of prayer because we are all capable of love. "It is only the devil," he says, "who is incapable of prayer because he is incapable of love."

Although prayer is a gift of God, something initiated by God, it is the way that we go to God. For our saint, it is something that is not merely confined to certain specific times of the day but must encompass our entire life from the very moment that we awaken until we take our rest at night and even when we awaken at night. St. Jane de Chantal, his very close friend and confidant, has captured this idea: "The essence of prayer is not in being always on our knees, but in keeping our will united to God's no matter what happens" (Conf. 36; *Works* 2:353–54).

THE SALESIAN
SPIRIT

What many people find very attractive about St. Francis de Sales is the spirit with which he conveys his teachings and how he carried these out in his own life. It is an affable, optimistic, balanced and encouraging spirit—one that is intent in winning hearts and not in winning arguments. This spirit becomes abundantly clear in his many Lenten sermons that have the essential aim of making our lives conform to that of the humble and gentle Jesus. It is exhibited in all of his writings, his letters, sermons, and in *Introduction to a Devout Life* and *Treatise on the Love of God.* The affable quality of his spirit emanates from his deep love and friendship with the Lord, whom he presents as readily accommodating himself to all in an endearing fashion.

His optimism flows from his Christian humanism, which is an understanding of our human nature based on Sacred Scripture, the Fathers of the Church, the writers of classical antiquity and personal experience. This humanism is rooted in the humanity of Jesus as the ideal for all human beings and in the truth that we are made in the image and likeness of God. He believes that we are born flawed but destined by our nature to love God above all things, namely, that we are naturally "wired" for God. Two examples come to mind that demonstrate this optimistic spirit. First, he believed that perfection consists in fighting against our imperfections and that as long as we are willing to fight, then we are always winners and never losers. This is a vision of perfection or holiness that everyone can readily identify with. Our saint also has a very optimistic view of sin: "Sin is shameful only when we commit it; when it has been converted by confession and repentance it becomes honorable and salutary" (*IDL*, pt. 1, ch. 19).

Our saint presents to us a balanced spirituality, one that Elisabeth Stopp has dubbed as "inspired commonsense." Many ideas and practices that he proposes appear to be eminently reasonable and doable. This is particularly seen when he warns us against excesses whether on the natural level or supernatural level. And so he counsels moderation in all things except the love of God. This is not to say that his spirituality is not demanding. It is very demanding because it makes demands more on our interior dispositions rather than on the practice of exterior austerities, which, at times, do not touch and change our hearts. So he sees that eating what is set before us can make greater demands on us than fasting because by it we mortify our choice which is one of the most difficult things for us to do. Of course, if what is set before us can make us ill, then he reasonably does not require us to follow this advice. This demonstrates his balanced approach.

Finally, his spirituality is very encouraging because he realized how discouragement can readily sap our spiritual energy. This encouraging spirit is especially seen in his advice on how to be gentle toward ourselves. Many people, "when overcome by anger," he remarks, "become angry at being angry, disturbed at being disturbed, and vexed at being vexed" (*IDL*, pt. 3, ch. 9). He tells us to be patient and compassionate toward ourselves when we commit a fault and not to lose heart over our many failings because our misery is the throne of God's mercy. We can appreciate how this affable, optimistic, balanced and encouraging spirit can readily seduce and win over the human heart and exhibits the saint's spirit, a spirit that we will find in many of his reflections on the Lenten gospels.

ON THE DAILY GOSPEL READINGS

As noted, this book presents daily readings and prayers for every day of Lent, weekdays and Sundays. The daily readings begin with a Gospel Reading, followed by a selection from St. Francis de Sales's writings, a reflection, and a prayer.

The Gospel Readings are from the Roman Catholic *Lectionary for Mass for Use in the Dioceses of the United States of America.* The *Lectionary* for Mass contains the readings for Mass selected from the Bible.

If you were to attend daily Mass during Lent in the United States, you would hear the same Daily Gospel Readings included in this book. For example, the Ash Wednesday Gospel Reading, Matthew 6:1–6, 16–18, is the same Gospel Reading you would hear when you attend Mass to receive your ashes. In fact, on each day at all the Masses of the Latin-rite Roman Catholic Church throughout the world, the same readings are heard in Mass, read in the vernacular language or Latin.

There are two main components of the Lectionary: Sunday and Weekday readings. Sunday readings are arranged on a three-year cycle: Year A, Year B, and Year C. The Gospel Readings for Year A are generally from the Gospel of St. Matthew, Year B are generally from the Gospel of St. Mark, and Year C are generally from the Gospel of St. Luke. St. John's Gospel is read on Sundays in Year A, B, and C during specific liturgical calendar periods.

The Weekday readings are on a two-year cycle: Year I and Year II. Year I are odd-numbered years and Year II are even-numbered years. The Weekday readings during Lent are the same for Year I and Year II although each day's reading is different. In the book, the Weekday Gospel Readings are also the Weekday Gospel Readings in the Lectionary.

For Sundays in this book, you have three different selections of readings and prayers. Each selection begins with a different Gospel Reading, the Gospel Reading from Year A, B, or C of the Lectionary.

Appendix A, the Calendar for Lent 2010–2019 & Lectionary Cycle, lists the specific dates for the next ten years for Ash Wednesday, the Sundays of Lent, and includes the Sunday Lectionary Cycle for the year. Please refer to the table to determine the current year's Sunday Lectionary Cycle: Year A, B, or C and select the appropriate Sunday reading for the present year.

This book in a small way invites you to pray each day with the Church and your fellow Christians in the world on your Lenten journey with Jesus Christ and St. Francis de Sales.

PETER J. MONGEAU

"Lent is the autumn of the spiritual life when we pick the fruit and gather it for the whole year. Enrich yourself, I beg you, with these precious treasures which nothing can neither steal nor destroy. . . . We never do well a Lenten season while thinking of doing two of them. So let us do this one as if it were our last one and we will do it well" (*OEA*, 13:144).

St. Francis de Sales

ASH
WEDNESDAY
and the Days
after Ash Wednesday

GOSPEL

JESUS SAID TO HIS DISCIPLES:

"Take care not to perform righteous deeds in order that people may see them; otherwise, you will have no recompense from your heavenly Father. When you give alms, do not blow a trumpet before you, as the hypocrites do in the synagogues and in the streets to win the praise of others. Amen, I say to you, they have received their reward. But when you give alms, do not let your left hand know what your right is doing, so that your almsgiving may be secret. And your Father who sees in secret will repay you.

"When you pray, do not be like the hypocrites, who love to stand and pray in the synagogues and on street corners so that others may see them. Amen, I say to you, they have received their reward. But when you pray, go to your inner room, close the door, and pray to your Father in secret. And your Father who sees in secret will repay you.

"When you fast, do not look gloomy like the hypocrites. They neglect their appearance, so that they may appear to others to be fasting. Amen, I say to you, they have received their reward. But when you fast, anoint your head and wash your face, so that you may not appear to be fasting, except to your Father who is hidden. And your Father who sees what is hidden will repay you."

MATTHEW 6: 1-6, 16-18

ST. FRANCIS DE SALES

"On the first day, [the Church] addresses us in these words: 'Remember . . . you are dust and into dust you shall return [Gen. 3:19] as if she meant to say: 'Quit at this moment all joyful and pleasant reflection, and fill you memory with bitter, hard and sorrowful thoughts. In this way, you will make your mind fast together with your body'" (Lenten Sermons, 3–4).

REFLECTION

"It is not enough to fast exteriorly if we do not also fast interiorly and if we do not accompany the fast of the body with that of the spirit. . . . [Our Lord] knew that to draw strength and efficacy from fasting, something more than abstinence from prohibited food is necessary. Thus he instructed them and, consequently, disposed them to gather the fruits proper to fasting. Among many others are these four: fasting fortifies the spirit, mortifying the flesh and its sensuality; it raises the spirit to God; it fights concupiscence and gives power to conquer and deaden the passions; in short, it disposes the heart to seek to please only God with great purity of heart" (*Lenten Sermons*, 2).

Fasting in itself is not a virtue. Religious and non-religious people fast for various reasons. Many in our society fast or go on reduced diets to lose weight for reasons of health or vanity. Fasting for a Christian must have the proper motivation. As our saint suggests, it must primarily be done to please God; otherwise, it will not contribute to our spiritual growth. Fasting, in his view, is much more than denying or limiting the physical food we eat but should be extended to disciplining our whole body and our spirit, that is, it is to be both interior and exterior. It involves keeping a close watch over our eyes, ears and mouths as well as our hearts.

We must be careful not to fast or perform other religious exercises so as to win the approval of others or display them before others because this defeats their very purpose and goal, namely, to strengthen our awareness of and ties to the Lord and others. Acts of self-denial are not to be performed primarily to attain self-mastery or self-control; they are intended to open our hearts more willingly and more promptly to God's love. So if denying ourselves certain foods or certain pleasures during Lent makes us grumpy and grouchy and difficult to live with, this kind of fasting runs counter to the very purpose of why the Church has us fast during the Lenten season. Our acts of self-denial should make us more affable, kind and considerate.

PRAYER

"Lord, here is this wretched heart of mine, which through your goodness has conceived many good affections. Alas, it is too weak and miserable to do the good that it desires to do unless you impart your heavenly blessing. For this purpose I humbly beg your blessing, O merciful Father, through the merits and passion of your Son, in whose honor I consecrate this day and all the remaining days of my life" (*IDL*, pt. 2, ch. 10). Amen.

GOSPEL

JESUS SAID TO HIS DISCIPLES:

"The Son of Man must suffer greatly and be rejected by the elders, the chief priests, and the scribes, and be killed and on the third day be raised."

Then he said to all, "If anyone wishes to come after me, he must deny himself and take up his cross daily and follow me. For whoever wishes to save his life will lose it, but whoever loses his life for my sake will save it. What profit is there for one to gain the whole world yet lose or forfeit himself?"

LUKE 9: 22-25

ST. FRANCIS DE SALES

"The merit of the cross does not consist in its heaviness, but in the manner in which we carry it. I would even say that it is sometimes more virtuous to carry a cross of straw than a heavy cross because we have to be more attentive for fear of losing it" (OEA, 9:19).

REFLECTION

Like his apostles, we find it difficult to accept Jesus' prediction of his suffering and death. The reason is that we instinctively recoil from and avoid pain and suffering because in and of themselves they are not something good. This is why normally we try to find relief from our suffering and pain. However, in this world, we will inevitably experience and endure suffering of one kind or another, whether it be physical, psychological or spiritual. We can only make sense out of it by joining our suffering to that of Jesus. It is Jesus who has made suffering redemptive. Our suffering can be redemptive and lead to eternal life when we take up our cross, when we accept, in the spirit of pleasing God, those trials, sufferings, disappointments, frustrations, and limitations that we daily have to deal with and cannot escape. "These little daily acts of charity, this headache, toothache, or cold, this bad [mood] in a husband or wife, this broken glass, this contempt or that scorn, this loss of a pair of gloves, ring, handkerchief, the little inconveniences incurred by going to bed early and getting up early to pray or receive Holy Communion, that little feeling of shame one has in performing certain acts of devotion in public—in short, all such little trials when accepted with love are highly pleasing to God's mercy" (*IDL*, pt. 3, ch. 35). Our saint would call the daily annoyances of one kind or another that we experience crosses of straw. Since these seem small, trivial and insignificant, we must be all the more aware of carrying them more attentively for fear of losing them.

Love and suffering go hand-in-hand. When we love the Lord deeply and faithfully, we will certainly encounter our share of suffering in the giving of ourselves to others out of love. "The merit of the cross," our saint observes, "does not consist in its heaviness, but in the manner in which we carry it. I would even say that it is sometimes more virtuous to carry a cross of straw than a heavy cross because we have to be more attentive for fear of losing it." These crosses of straw come in the form of little daily annoyances when things do not go our way and cause a good deal of frustration because of their frequency. It is in bearing these small crosses that we come to test the kind of person the Lord wants us to become. So paradoxically, by attentively and lovingly carrying our crosses, we do not lose ourselves but actually find our true selves and our true destiny.

PRAYER

Lord, help me to overcome my reluctance to suffering and make me understand the necessary connection between love, suffering and the cross. In this way, I will be encouraged to join my suffering with yours so that in dying to my selfish inclinations, I may rise to a new and invigorating life with you. Grant this in the name of Jesus, your Son and our Brother. Amen.

GOSPEL

The disciples of John approached Jesus and said, "Why do we and the Pharisees fast much, but your disciples do not fast?" Jesus answered them, "Can the wedding guests mourn as long as the bridegroom is with them? The days will come when the bridegroom is taken away from them, and then they will fast."

MATTHEW 9: 14-15

ST. FRANCIS DE SALES

"Oh, these preachers! They forbid every joy, every food, every smile, every care for temporal goods. They want us to be in Church all day long, fasting. Ah! They are the traitors of humanity! We do not say this, but rather, nourish yourself with every joy, but do not use the joy of sin" (OEA, 8:82–83).

REFLECTION

It is interesting to note that the disciples of John and not the scribes and the Pharisees question Jesus why his disciples do not fast. In those days, those who were serious about the practice of their religious faith were recognized by prayer, fasting and the giving of alms—three religious practices considered to be the cornerstone of the Jewish religion. Fasting was especially valued as a means of demonstrating one's dedication to God and also as a sign of mourning. Jesus' reply gives evidence of a deep understanding of the Jewish culture. This culture placed a high value on the special festive occasion of a wedding celebration, which lasted for several days. He tells his questioners that fasting, would be totally out of place during a wedding feast, where there is supposed to be joy and not sadness. In referring to himself as the bridegroom, Jesus reveals himself to be the Messiah, whose presence is implicitly compared to an extravagant wedding celebration.

Since our saint, as noted above, understood fasting in a much wider sense, he sees occasions for practicing an extended notion of fasting even among great festivity. For example, we can eat what is set before us even if we do not particularly care for a certain dish, as long as it does not make us ill. This interior kind of fasting is very difficult to do because it involves sacrificing our choice, something that we give up with great difficulty. Furthermore, it does not bring attention to ourselves and does not inconvenience anyone. Another form of fasting amid festive or any kind of gathering is to be pleasant and agreeable to other table guests who might be difficult or uncivil. So for our saint, a more interior kind fasting, which can be practiced in all kinds of public settings, can actually make more demands on us than the conventional way of fasting.

PRAYER

Give us, Father, a deeper understanding of the notion of fasting. In this way, we will be able to discipline ourselves out of love for you in all kinds of social settings. This will no doubt make greater demands on us but happily make us more attentive to your nuptial presence among us. Grant this through Jesus Christ, Our Lord. Amen.

GOSPEL

Jesus saw a tax collector named Levi sitting at the customs post. He said to him, "Follow me." And leaving everything behind, he got up and followed him. Then Levi gave a great banquet for him in his house, and a large crowd of tax collectors and others were at table with them. The Pharisees and their scribes complained to his disciples, saying, "Why do you eat and drink with tax collectors and sinners?" Jesus said to them in reply, "Those who are healthy do not need a physician, but the sick do. I have not come to call the righteous to repentance but sinners."

LUKE 5: 27-32

ST. FRANCIS DE SALES

"God does not always choose the holiest to govern and to have charges in his Church. Therefore, those who are called ought not to glorify themselves and presume themselves to be more perfect than others. And those who receive such offices ought not to be troubled about it, since that will not prevent them from being just and pleasing to God" (Lenten Sermons, *80–81).*

REFLECTION

The choices that Jesus makes of his apostles may appear to us as strange and bizarre. Why would he want to have a tax-collector, who very likely was involved in all kinds of shady and dishonest dealings, become one of those upon whom he would build his Church? Well, scripture answers that for us when we read that "God's ways are not our ways" (Is. 55:89). We see how readily Levi responds to God's call. He does not ask any questions; he does not say that he can't just drop everything. He gets up and leaves everything behind to begin a new, exhilarating and exciting life.

Despite all of his wealth, Levi must have experienced a deep void in his life and said to himself many times: "Is that all there is?" He must have felt in his heart of hearts that Jesus was the only one who could fill this void, this distressing emptiness. The sumptuous banquet that he throws, inviting all of his cronies or whom we may call "partners in crime," gives evidence of how promptly, joyfully, and trustingly he responded to Jesus' call. It is a reminder to us of how transforming God's grace can be if only we respond to it generously and lovingly. We should find great comfort in Jesus' response to his critics about associating with despised tax-collectors and sinners. He is the physician who has specifically come to heal our spiritual illness since we are all sinners and have desperate need of him.

PRAYER

"[Father], I do have needs; I am wounded by many sins, and I need remedies. You, Father, are the physician who heals all my ills and cures all my infirmities [see Ps. 103:3; Mt. 4:23]. Have mercy on me, Lord, for I am weak; heal me, Lord, for my bones are trembling"[Ps. 6:3], and I shall be healed. Lord, heal this soul; see how it comes before you full of wounds . . . of pride, avarice, lust, etc. and lovingly asks for health"(OEA, 26:388–89). Amen.

QUESTIONS FOR REFLECTION
OR DISCUSSION

1. What are your ideas and experiences of prayer and how do they compare with those of St. Francis de Sales?

2. How helpful do you find a method of meditation?

3. What do you think of St. Francis de Sales' suggestion that "A good way to accustom ourselves to making these ejaculations is to take the petitions of the Our Father one after another, choosing a sentence for each day"?

4. Why does St. Francis de Sales find it so important for us to exercise self-discipline and self-denial?

5. In what ways can you practice mortifying your choice?

FIRST WEEK
OF
LENT

GOSPEL

At that time Jesus was led by the Spirit into the desert to be tempted by the devil. He fasted for forty days and forty nights, and afterwards he was hungry. The tempter approached and said to him, "If you are the Son of God, command that these stones become loaves of bread."

He said in reply, "It is written: / *One does not live on bread alone,* / *but on every word that comes forth from the mouth of God.*" / Then the devil took him to the holy city, and made him stand on the parapet of the temple, and said to him, "If you are the Son of God, throw yourself down. For it is written: / *He will command his angels concerning you* / *and with their hands they will support you,* / *lest you dash your foot against a stone.*" / Jesus answered him, "Again it is written, *You shall not put the Lord, your God, to the test.*" Then the devil took him up to a very high mountain, and showed him all the kingdoms of the world in their magnificence, and he said to him, "All these I shall give to you, if you will prostrate yourself and worship me." At this, Jesus said to him, "Get away, Satan! It is written: / *The Lord, your God, shall you worship* / *and him alone shall you serve.*" / Then the devil left him and, behold, angels came and ministered to him.

MATTHEW 4: 1-11

ST. FRANCIS DE SALES

"Fear is the first temptation which the enemy presents to those who have resolved to serve God, for as soon as they are shown what perfection requires of them they think, 'Alas, I shall never be able to do it'" (Lenten Sermons, *19).*

REFLECTION

As we set out on this Lenten journey, we can count on being set upon by temptations. These come in various forms and at unsuspecting times. The most common might be a lack of interest, of perseverance, or perhaps of mistakenly believing that we simply do not have the time to spend on reading and reflecting on the Lenten Gospels. At times, we may be deprived of any good feelings and consolations and believe that we are really having a desert experience. This can prove to be very valuable for a number of reasons. It can help us center and focus our lives on Jesus and the things that really matter rather than to pursue power, prestige and recognition. Furthermore, it can give a sense of our inadequacy that emboldens us to seek and find our adequacy and strength in God alone as we reflect and meditate on the true meaning of the sacred word. This can lead us to gain a deeper understanding of ourselves—of our strengths and weaknesses, of our brokenness and blessings—and what the Lord expects from us. Whenever we decide to get more serious about our faith, especially during Lent, we can count on the evil spirit attempting to convince us in so many ways, subtle and not so subtle, that we are too hopelessly flawed or lacking in strength of will and determination. Perhaps, we may even believe that we're pretty good persons and don't need all of this extra effort and bother. It is at those times, that we especially have to reflect on Jesus' experience as he set out on the mission his Father gave him and how he courageously and victoriously withstood the blandishments of the devil. His victory over the evil one has won for us the courage and determination we need to successfully deal with the devil's temptations.

PRAYER

May we, Lord, "fear neither the temptation nor the tempter." We trust that at such times, you will provide us "with the shield of faith and the armor of truth" (*Lenten Sermons*, 32). These will give us the courage to endure and overcome the temptation and thus make us aware of how close you are to us and how much you care for and guide us on our journey. We ask this in Jesus' name. Amen.

GOSPEL

The Spirit drove Jesus out into the desert, and he remained in the desert for forty days, tempted by Satan. He was among wild beasts, and the angels ministered to him.

After John had been arrested, Jesus came to Galilee proclaiming the gospel of God: "This the time of fulfillment. The kingdom of God is at hand. Repent, and believe in the gospel."

MARK 1: 12-15

ST. FRANCIS DE SALES

"Just as the desire for paradise is worthy of the most honor so also fear of damnation is of the greatest value. Not only that, but since desire of paradise is of great worth, fear of its contrary, which is hell, is good and praiseworthy. Ah, who would not fear so great a loss and so great a torment! These two fears of which one is servile and the other mercenary are powerful means bringing us to repent of our sins whereby we have incurred them. It is for such effect that fear is brought home to us hundreds and hundreds of times in Sacred Scripture" (TLG, I:150–51).

REFLECTION

Lent is the time to create sacred space in our lives. The testing of Jesus and his fasting in the desert are the example given to us whereby we can create this sacred space. Fasting whether it be from food or drink or from many of our selfish and self-centered impulses helps to make room in our hearts for God and his word. Repentance for our past sins removes the baggage that clutters up our lives and makes us take responsibility for ourselves and the consequences of our ill-considered free choices. Furthermore, repentance reorients our lives away from self toward God by helping us realize and work on what comes between us and the Lord. Repentance turns the water of our tears into the wine of his divine love. The basic message that Jesus preaches is intended to make us more aware of the presence of God's kingdom among us and within us. By self-discipline and a change of heart regarding our past sins, we become all the more receptive to serving and promoting the kingdom of God, where the good news of love, mercy and forgiveness reign in the person of Jesus and in his body, the Church.

PRAYER

"'Thy kingdom come.' Here, Father, in my body and soul is your kingdom. You desire to reign in this kingdom. I surrender it to you, Oh Father; I give it to you. May it be truly yours since it really is yours. May I not usurp it, may I not deliver it up to Satan, to the world nor to the flesh, which are cruel tyrants, but to you who is its true Lord. So, Father, your kingdom come. Reign from now on in my soul, in my memory so that it remembers you always, in my understanding so that it always considers your infinite goodness and grandeur, in my will so that it may unceasingly love, praise and bless you" (*OEA*, 26:405).

GOSPEL

Filled with the Holy Spirit, Jesus returned from the Jordan and was led by the Spirit into the desert for forty days, to be tempted by the devil. He ate nothing during those days, and when they were over he was hungry. The devil said to him, "If you are the Son of God, command this stone to become bread." Jesus answered him, "It is written, *One does not live on bread alone."* Then he took him up and showed him all the kingdoms of the world in a single instant. The devil said to him, "I shall give to you all this power and glory; for it has been handed over to me, and I may give it to whomever I wish. All this will be yours, if you worship me." Jesus said to him in reply, "It is written: / *You shall worship the Lord, your God, and him alone shall you serve."* / Then he led them to Jerusalem, made him stand on the parapet of the temple, and said to him, "If you are the Son of God, throw yourself down from here, for it is written: / *He will command his angels concerning you, to guard you,* / and: / *With their hands they will support you, / lest you dash your foot against a stone."* / Jesus said to him in reply, "It also says, *You shall not put the Lord, your God, to the test."* When the devil had finished every temptation, he departed from him for a time.

LUKE 4: 1-13

ST. FRANCIS DE SALES

"Do not seek for other arms or weapons in order to refuse consent to any temptation except to say, 'I believe.' And what do you believe? 'In God,' my 'Father Almighty'" (Lenten Sermons, 19).

REFLECTION

Being alone in the desert is meant to convey a religious experience that forces us to come to grips with our basic identity and mission in life, as it did for Jesus. To undergo this kind of self-examination leads us open to many temptations that easily lead us in the wrong direction. The desert experience is a time when we strip ourselves of every other concern so as to concentrate on the essentials. That is why there is a feeling of barrenness, of sterility, of being terribly alone. It is a time when we face honestly and squarely good and evil and make the kinds of choices that influence the direction our lives will take. It is a time for us to confront our deep-seated hungers and ask ourselves what is it that we most hunger for or desire. Are we tempted primarily to seek physical and material security by telling ourselves that we are simply pursuing these things to be better off? Here is what Peter Maurin says about those who just want to be better off:

> The world would be better off
> if people tried to become better
> and people would become better
> if they stopped trying to become better off.
> For when everyone tries to become
> better off nobody is better off
> But when everyone tries to become better
> everyone is better off.[1]

---

1. Cited by Wendy Wright in *Seasons of a Family Life: Cultivating the Contemplative Spirit at Home* (San Francisco: Jossey-Bass, 2003), 99.

Do we sincerely believe with the Lord Jesus that these things are insufficient and that we must strive to live and be nourished by the word of God? Jesus' desert experience cautions us not to succumb to the temptation that political activity, as important as it may be, is the most effective way of achieving true freedom and justice for the needy and the marginalized. As followers of the Lord Jesus, we are certainly called to be risk-takers, but we must be careful of not giving in to the temptation of taking imprudent or ill-advised risks that are merely for show to make us look good and endanger our spiritual journey and our spiritual lives.

PRAYER

"We are, Oh Father, in a place of temptation. Our adversary, the devil prowls among us looking for someone to devour [see 1 Peter 5:8]. Give me the wherewithal, help me, Oh Father. My enemies are as numerous as the sands of the sea and experienced in combat. My soul is weak, languishing, powerless if you do not come to my aid. . . . Oh Lord, how much this poor soul needs your grace, your help, your assistance so as not to succumb to temptations" (*OEA*, 26:415). Amen.

GOSPEL

JESUS SAID TO HIS DISCIPLES:

"When the Son of Man comes in his glory, and all the angels with him, he will sit upon his glorious throne, and all the nations will be assembled before him. And he will separate them one from another, as a shepherd separates the sheep from the goats. He will place the sheep on his right and the goats on his left. Then the king will say to those on his right, 'Come, you who are blessed by my Father. Inherit the kingdom prepared for you from the foundation of the world. For I was hungry and you gave me food, I was thirsty and you gave me drink, a stranger and you welcomed me, naked and you clothed me, ill and you cared for me, in prison and you visited me.' Then the righteous will answer him and say, 'Lord, when did we see you hungry and feed you, or thirsty and give you drink? When did we see you a stranger and welcome you, or naked and clothe you? When did we see you ill or in prison, and visit you?' And the king will say to them in reply, 'Amen, I say to you, whatever you did for one of these least brothers of mine, you did for me.' Then he will say to those on his left, 'Depart from me, you accursed, into the eternal fire prepared for the Devil and his angels. For I was hungry and you gave me no food, I was thirsty and you gave me no drink, a stranger and you gave me no welcome, naked and you gave me no clothing, ill and in prison, and you did not care for me.' Then they will answer and say, 'Lord, when did we see you hungry or thirsty or a stranger or naked or ill or in prison, and not minister to your needs?' He will answer them, 'Amen, I say to you, what you did not do for one of these least ones, you did not do for me.' And these will go off to eternal punishment, but the righteous to eternal life."

MATTHEW 25: 31-46

ST. FRANCIS DE SALES

"No one is to excuse himself from this and say that he does not know that he is to love his neighbor as himself, because God has imprinted this truth in the bottom of our hearts in creating all of us in the image and likeness of each other. Bearing the image of God in ourselves, all of us are consequently the image of each other. Together we constitute the image of one portrait, that of God" (Lenten Sermons, *88).*

REFLECTION

What we do or do not do really matters and has consequences both for good and for evil. In the framework of the final judgment, Jesus is stressing accountability for our actions and the necessity of love and compassion. These virtues, of course, can only be expressed in our relationships with other human beings who have a direct bearing on our relationship with God. As one writer puts it, "Relation to God is by necessity lived out in relation to humans."[1] Performing these acts of kindness for needy human beings makes us not only encounter them, but also God in whose image we are all created. For our saint, this truth is at the very heart of his understanding of who we are, and for whom we are. Kind and compassionate actions give us our sense of self-identity, and, by connecting with others in this way, we also connect with God. It is by loving and giving of ourselves to others that we become who we are, persons created by love for love. The more loving we become, the more human we become. So love and compassion not only humanize us but also, in a sense divinize us, that is, make us more Godlike. On the other hand, when we do not connect with others in need with love and compassion, then we disconnect with God and seriously compromise and diminish our humanity.

PRAYER

Lord, your servant Francis de Sales was fond of saying that since we are all made in the image of God, then we are all made in the image of one another. Help us to readily recognize and respond to this image, especially in those who are least likely to reflect it, so that we may not only lovingly connect with them but also with you for all eternity. We ask this in Jesus' name. Amen.

---

1. Klyne R. Snodgrass, *Stories With Intent: A Comprehensive Guide to the Parables of Jesus* (Grand Rapids, MI.: Eerdmans, 2008), 560.

GOSPEL

JESUS SAID TO HIS DISCIPLES:

"In praying, do not babble like the pagans, who think that they will be heard because of their many words. Do not be like them. Your Father knows what you need before you ask him.

"This is how you are to pray:

Our Father who art in heaven,
hallowed be thy name,
thy Kingdom come,
thy will be done,
on earth as it is in heaven.
Give us this day our daily bread;
and forgive us our trespasses,
as we forgive those who trespass against us;
and lead us not into temptation,
but deliver us from evil.

"If you forgive men their transgressions, your heavenly Father will forgive you. But if you do not forgive men, neither will your Father forgive your transgressions."

MATTHEW 6: 7-15

ST. FRANCIS DE SALES

"In these two words, 'Our Father,' you reveal to me, Lord, another great mystery, namely, that you desire that I greatly love your holy law of love and of charity, for you have reduced it all to love of you and love of our neighbor. By the first word, 'Father,' you ask me to love your most supreme majesty, by the second, 'Our,' you ask me to love my neighbor since you give him to me as a brother and you desire that I pray for him" (OEA, 26:394).

REFLECTION

"Oh eternal Father, Father of our Lord Jesus Christ, 'Father of Lights,' [Jas. 1:17] holy Father, all gentle and all loving Father, Father creator of the universe, how can I ever deserve to call you 'Father,' I who am earthly, 'dust and ashes' [Gen. 18:27] the least of all your servants? What possible good have you found in me or in any other child of Adam that you desired to be our Father? 'Who are you Lord and who am I?' [St. Francis of Assisi, *Speculum vitae*]. You are the God of infinite majesty, the 'King of kings, Lord of Lords' [Rev. 17:14, 19:16], the Saint of saints, the glory of the angels and joy of all the blessed. In your sight, the heavens, the earth and all it contains are less than a small grain of sand in comparison to the whole world. But I, on the other hand, am a little earthworm, a sinner and a child of sinful Adam, who has so often offended your sovereign majesty. And yet, you want me to call you Father! Oh! What excellence, what dignity you give me! May it please you, Lord, that my soul come to recognize this and give you the thanks due to so great a blessing. But since my gratitude is insufficient, I pray that the angels assist me in praising and thanking you unceasingly.

"Father, I must confess two things: one that this gift and great blessing comes from your infinite goodness and the infinite love you have for me, the other that this word Father is so fitting on the lips of your only Son, my Lord Jesus Christ, who is your Son by an eternal and consubstantial generation, but on my lips, I who am such a great sinner, it is not fitting, it is not appropriate. I do not deserve such a great blessing. Nevertheless, since it so pleases your majesty, with all my heart, I shall from now on call you Father, and I will rejoice in this sweet name of Father.

"This word gives testimony to the immense love that you have for me, Lord. This is why your evangelist, filled with amazement, says: 'See what love the Father has for us that we are called children of God and so we really are' [1 Jn. 3:1]. It also teaches and equally informs me that I must love you with my whole heart: 'I love you, Lord, my strength, my rock, my refuge, my liberator' [Ps. 18:2, 3] and my Father. What ungrateful son could there possibly be in the world, who having such a good, holy, gentle, glorious and loving Father as you, would not love him?" (*OEA*, 26:388).

PRAYER

"I beg you . . . Oh Father, to give me the sufficient strength and your grace so that I may completely forgive those who have offended me, and if you find in my heart some imperfection inimical to those who have offended me, grant, Father, that you may make it disappear by the fire of you charity. Burn it, grant that not a trace or a hint of bitterness remain in my heart so that I may say in all truth: 'Forgive our offenses as we forgive those who have offended us'" (*OEA*,26:414). Amen.

GOSPEL

While still more people gathered in the crowd, Jesus said to them, "This generation is an evil generation; it seeks a sign, but no sign will be given it, except the sign of Jonah. Just as Jonah became a sign to the Ninevites, so will the Son of Man be to this generation. At the judgment the queen of the south will rise with the men of this generation and she will condemn them, because she came from the ends of the earth to hear the wisdom of Solomon, and there is something greater than Solomon here. At the judgment the men of Nineveh will arise with this generation and condemn it, because at the preaching of Jonah they repented, and there is something greater than Jonah here."

LUKE 11: 29-32

ST. FRANCIS DE SALES

"Attentive faith is very great and excellent. In addition to being living and vigilant, it attains the highest point of perfection through this attentiveness" (Lenten Sermons, *41).*

REFLECTION

It is a common human experience to miss the significance of events that occur under our very noses. The principal reason for this appears to be our distractedness or our unwillingness to live in the present moment. We seem to be looking for extraordinary things to happen in our daily life and fail to appreciate the value and significance of the seemingly ordinary things we encounter day-in-and-day out. Despite all of the many kind and merciful actions that Jesus performed before their very eyes, the religious leaders of his day were slow to understand their meaning and to look beyond these signs to the one significant sign of the person who accomplished all of these compassionate actions. No wonder Jesus became impatient with them and bluntly told them, that they have a sufficient number of signs of his divine mission and power.

To emphasize to them how obtuse they were, he cites the story of Jonah's preaching repentance to the Ninevites and the Queen of Sheba's great admiration for the wisdom of Solomon. The point Jesus is making is that those not particularly favored by God, namely the despised Ninevites and a gentile Queen, were more responsive to God working among them than they were. They failed to see in his very person, in his preaching and in his many healings, the power, presence and love of God working in their midst. In particular, this Gospel passage stresses how readily the Ninevites responded to the sign of Jonah's preaching and repented of their sins.

We need to reflect on the many signs of God's goodness and blessings we encounter in those who love us and sacrifice for us. These should be the signs that make us conscious of God working in our lives and of our lack of appreciation; they should make us more aware of our shortcomings and our sinfulness that should lead us to a sincere and a life-transforming repentance. Moreover, this conversion will enable us to more readily see the sign of Jesus' presence in others and with our saint make the following resolution: "I will never disdain meeting any person, no matter who they may not be, nor will I show any sign of wishing to avoid them. . . . I will be careful neither to criticize, nor to mock, nor to be sarcastic to anyone. . . . I will show great respect to all, and I will not be pretentious. I will speak little but well, so rather than boring my friends I will whet their appetite for further conversation at a later time" (*Spiritual Exercises*, 36–37).

PRAYER

Time and time again, dear Lord, you have demonstrated your presence and love in my life in so many ordinary and unsuspecting ways. Yet, I have so often been too slow to acknowledge, praise and thank you for these blessings. Sharpen the eyes of my faith that I may be more aware of the many signs of your presence in my life and the lives of others. Grant this through Jesus Christ your Son. Amen.

GOSPEL

JESUS SAID TO HIS DISCIPLES:

"Ask and it will be given to you; seek and you will find; knock and the door will be opened to you. For everyone who asks, receives; and the one who seeks, finds; and to the one who knocks, the door will be opened. Which one of you would hand his son a stone when he asked for a loaf of bread, or a snake when he asked for a fish? If you then, who are wicked, know how to give good gifts to your children, how much more will your heavenly Father give good things to those who ask him.

"Do to others whatever you would have them do to you. This is the law and the prophets."

MATTHEW 7: 7-12

ST. FRANCIS DE SALES

"This word, 'Father,' moves me to ask you for the things I need, for a father never refuses his child what he sees is necessary, provided he can give it to him. I know, my Father, that you can and will; you can because you are omnipotent; you will because you are all good" (OEA, 26:388).

REFLECTION

The basic motivation for our prayers of petition finds its source in the picture that Jesus and the scriptures paint of God as our merciful, loving and caring Father. Our God is not a God who dwells on a distant and inaccessible Mount Olympus wrapped in indifference and heavenly isolation, but one who is well aware of our needs and well-disposed to grant them just as any human father who cares deeply for his children. This belief and confidence in our fatherly God made a deep impression on our saint so that he exclaims: "This word, Father, moves me to ask you for the things I need, for a father never refuses his child what he sees is necessary, provided he can give it to him. I know, my Father, that you can and will; you can because you are omnipotent; you will because you are all good." How encouraging is Our Lord's admonition to ask, seek, and knock for the things we need from our heavenly Father. It is this assurance that we must rely on during our Lenten Journey as we become more aware of our spiritual needs and those of others who are near and dear to us. The more we become aware of our many needs, the more fervently, persistently and perseveringly must we cry out to our Father, who will answer us in due time and give us what will truly be for our good. Our saint urges us to ask incessantly for the Father's love and explains himself in this way: "Temporal avarice, whereby we avidly desire earthly treasures 'is the root of all evil,' [1 Tim. 6:10] but spiritual avarice whereby we unceasingly sigh for the pure gold of sacred love is the root of all good. One who truly desires love seeks it; he who truly seeks it finds it" (*TLG*, II: 263).

In our saint's view, our prayers of petition are particularly efficacious when we are joined to others in prayer under the guidance of the Holy Spirit and made in the name of Jesus, who has promised to be with us when we are gathered in his name. It is at the times of communal prayer that Jesus prays with and for us. And we know and believe that there is no prayer more pleasing to the Father than that of his only Son.

With regard to the golden rule enunciated in this Gospel passage, our saint understood our relationships with others as an excellent means of discerning God's will for us. He firmly believed that there is no better way of discovering God's will than the voice of my neighbor since God does not usually speak directly to us or through angels but through other human beings. So as we are aware of asking the Father for what we need, we should also be aware of what God wants and expects from us.

PRAYER

"Father full of compassion, remember that when little children ask their father for bread, especially if they are really hungry, they cry out with all their strength: 'Bread, Bread!' and with this word, like so many arrows, they wound the heart of their fathers who, here below, search for bread to give to their children. Here I am famished, Oh our Father. Listen to this word that I address to you: 'Some bread, Father, some bread! Deign, then, holy Father, open the bowels of your mercy, [see Lk. 1:78] and because you are able to, come to my aid and give your child the bread of your grace and the supersubstantial Bread of your Most Holy Sacrament'"(*OEA*, 26:410-11). Amen.

GOSPEL

JESUS SAID TO HIS DISCIPLES:

"I tell you, unless your righteousness surpasses that of the scribes and Pharisees, you will not enter into the Kingdom of heaven.

"You have heard that it was said to your ancestors, *You shall not kill; and whoever kills will be liable to judgment.* But I say to you, whoever is angry with his brother will be liable to judgment, and whoever says to his brother, *Raqa,* will be answerable to the Sanhedrin, and whoever says, 'You fool,' will be liable to fiery Gehenna. Therefore, if you bring your gift to the altar, and there recall that your brother has anything against you, leave your gift there at the altar, go first and be reconciled with your brother, and then come and offer your gift. Settle with your opponent quickly while on the way to court. Otherwise your opponent will hand you over to the judge, and the judge will hand you over to the guard, and you will be thrown into prison. Amen, I say to you, you will not be released until you have paid the last penny."

MATTHEW 5: 20-26

ST. FRANCIS DE SALES

"Let us purify our intention as far as we can. . . . Since we can diffuse throughout all the various acts the sacred motive of love, why should we not do so?" (TLG, II: 237).

REFLECTION

This passage emphasizes the ways in which Jesus completes or fulfills the law, the Torah. A number of the Pharisees made a public display of their religious practices in order to be seen and applauded by people. There is in all of us a pharisaical tendency to make a show of our faith by performing external actions without the proper motivation. This can easily turn religious practices into routine so that our heart is not really in them. The way that our saint helps us to overcome a merely external devotion is by urging us to perform all of our actions no matter how small and insignificant, out of love for God. It is in this way that our righteousness or holiness will exceed that of a merely legalistic and external form of religion.

In his *Treatise on the Love of God*, our saint illustrates the importance of the right motivation by an interesting story. There were two men who lived in the city of Antioch at the time of the emperors Valerian and Gallus. One of them, Sapricius, was a priest; the other named Nicephorus was a layman. They were such great, close friends that people looked upon them as brothers. For one reason or another, they had a falling out. As usually happens in such relationships, they had a great mutual hatred for each other. Later, Nicephorus sought reconciliation and sent words of apology to his former friend. But Sapricius ignored this overture "with pride as great as the humility with which Nicephorus sought it." So Nicephorus thought that if he would throw himself at Sapricius's feet asking forgiveness, that his former friend would be moved to forgive him. Well, this didn't work either. When a persecution broke out, Sapricius among others was arrested. As he was being led to be killed, Nicephorus again threw himself at Sapricius's feet begging him to forgive him out of love of God. But the priest remained adamant. Even at the place of execution, with Nicephorus again pleading for forgiveness at his feet, Sapricius refused obstinately to grant him pardon. Well, when it came time for the priest to kneel down to have his head chopped off, he lost courage and agreed to submit to the emperor.

The observation that our saint makes on this story is very illuminating: "Alas, that unfortunate priest came to the altar of martyrdom to consecrate his life to God eternal, but he was not mindful of what the prince of martyrs had said: 'If you are offering your gift at the altar, and there remember that your brother has anything against you, leave your gift there before the altar, and go first to be reconciled with your brother, and then return and offer your gift'" [Mt. 5:23] (*TLG*, II:163). Of course, the point of the story is that the priest's motivation was not love of God but essentially pride and vanity, which was revealed by the fact that he was not willing to forgive his former friend. Our saint's comment brings the point home all the more forcefully: "To be willing to die for God is the greatest but not the only act of [love] that we owe to God. To will this sole act while rejecting the rest is not charity; it is vanity. Charity is not folly, but it would be such in a superlative degree if it willed to please the beloved in the most difficult things and yet would let us displease him in easier matters. How can a man be willing to die for God if he is unwilling to live according to God?" (*TLG*, II:162–64).

PRAYER

Father, you know how easily we are inclined to make a show of our faith by seeking the approval and approbation of others. Help us to understand how essential it is to monitor closely the motives of all of our actions so that we perform them primarily to please you and not to please ourselves. In this way, we will come to appreciate what you expect our righteousness to be in your sight and grow in your love and mercy. We ask this in Jesus' name. Amen.

GOSPEL

JESUS SAID TO HIS DISCIPLES:

"You have heard that it was said, *You shall love your neighbor and hate your enemy.* But I say to you, love your enemies, and pray for those who persecute you, that you may be children of your heavenly Father, for he makes his sun rise on the bad and the good, and causes rain to fall on the just and the unjust. For if you love those who love you, what recompense will you have? Do not the tax collectors do the same? And if you greet your brothers and sisters only, what is unusual about that? Do not the pagans do the same? So be perfect, just as your heavenly Father is perfect."

MATTHEW 5: 43-48

ST. FRANCIS DE SALES

"God would sooner work miracles than leave us without assistance either spiritual or temporal, those who trust entirely in his Divine Providence. Yet he wants us, for our part, to do all that lies in our power, that is, he wants us to use ordinary means to attain perfection. If these should fail, he will never fail to assist us" (Lenten Sermons, *121*)

REFLECTION

The word perfection turns many people off because they think this means that we are to be flawless and sinless, and they just can't picture themselves in that way. Our saint realized this and tells us that perfection consists in fighting against our imperfections. As long as we are willing to fight, then we are winners and not losers. The greatest imperfection that we all have to struggle with is our tendency to be unloving or to naturally limit our love to those we like or those who like us or are friendly toward us. But to be his followers, Jesus plainly tells us that this is insufficient because it is not the way that God loves and the way that we are all called to love. So he raises the bar here by demonstrating how pervasive and all inclusive is God's love and how we are to mirror and reflect this love in our lives.

Many may have to struggle with the distorted concept they have of God, Our Father. The idea of God as a punisher and judge of our sins and faults looms very large and threateningly in a number of those who call themselves Christians. For them, God is seen primarily in the person of Christ as a kind of "bogeyman." This readily gives rise to routine religious practices intended to placate an irate God without any deep, moving experience of the living, loving, forgiving and merciful God. After all, who can get friendly with a bogeyman? We know that the Lord Jesus is the perfect "image of the invisible God" (Col. 1:15). In him God's love and forgiveness is reflected perfectly. We see in Jesus a God who loves passionately, recklessly and indiscriminately. He causes the rain to fall on the just and unjust; he livens ups a wedding party by miraculously providing excellent wine. Our God in Jesus reaches out to those who are hurting, heals the brokenhearted, shows great tenderness to children, raises the dead to life. This is the kind of God we are called to imitate; this is what it means to be "holy, as the Lord is holy," "to be perfect as the Father is perfect." We cannot imitate God in his omniscience and omnipotence, but we can imitate him in his kindness and compassion. These are the imitable traits of our perfect God; these are what we must strive to imitate. And God will provide the wherewithal to achieve this kind of "perfection," provided we are willing to struggle daily against our imperfections.

PRAYER

"I ask with insistence, Oh Father, that thy will be done in me and in everyone because I am certain that it is your will that everyone become saints. 'Be holy for I am holy' [Lev. 11:14; 1 Pet. 1:16]. 'This is my will, your sanctification' [1 Thess. 4:3]. Oh fountain of all holiness, make us holy for such is your will. What person can be so blind in understanding that he does not desire to be a saint? Holy Father, I don't look for nor desire anything else; my wealth, my possessions, my treasure will consist in being a saint. May thy will be done in me so that I may be a saint" (*OEA*, 26:407). Amen.

QUESTIONS FOR REFLECTION
OR DISCUSSION

1. In what sense would St. Francis de Sales agree that what we do tells us who we are?

2. How would you describe God to one who does not believe in God?

3. In what ways can you relate to St. Francis de Sales' concept of holiness or perfection as consisting in struggling against our imperfections?

4. What little daily occurrences remind you of God working in your life, in the lives of others and in our world?

5. How does St. Francis de Sales help us understand Jesus' saying that he has not come to "abolish the Law but to fulfill it"?

SECOND WEEK
OF
LENT

GOSPEL

Jesus took Peter, James, and John his brother, and led them up a high mountain by themselves. And he was transfigured before them; his face shone like the sun and his clothes became white as light. And behold, Moses and Elijah appeared to them, conversing with him. Then Peter said to Jesus in reply, "Lord, it is good that we are here. If you wish, I will make three tents here, one for you, one for Moses, and one for Elijah." While he was still speaking, behold, a bright cloud cast a shadow over them, then from the cloud came a voice that said, "This is my beloved Son, with whom I am well pleased; listen to him." When the disciples heard this, they fell prostrate and were very much afraid. But Jesus came and touched them, saying, "Rise, and do not be afraid." And when the disciples raised their eyes, they saw no one else but Jesus alone.

As they were coming down from the mountain, Jesus charged them, "Do not tell the vision to anyone until the Son of Man has been raised from the dead."

MATTHEW 17: 1-9

ST. FRANCIS DE SALES

"In this vision and clear knowledge consists the essence of felicity. There we will understand and participate in the adorable conversations and divine colloquies which take place between the Father, Son and Holy Spirit" (Lenten Sermons, *63*).

REFLECTION

"The apostles saw his face become more dazzling and brilliant than the sun. Indeed, this light and glory was spread even over his clothes to show us that it was so diffusive as to be shared by his very clothes and whatever was about him. He shows us a spark of eternal glory and a drop of that ocean, of that sea of incomprehensible felicity, to make us desire it in its entirety. So the good St. Peter, as head of the others, spoke for all and exclaimed in full joy and consolation: 'O how good it is for us to be here!' He seems to mean: 'I have seen many good things, but nothing is so desirable as remaining here.' The three disciples recognize Moses and Elias even though they had never seen them before . . . Let me remark first of all that we will know each other, since in this little spark of it which the Savior gave to the apostles, he willed that they recognize Moses and Elias, whom they had never seen. If this is true, O my God, what contentment will we receive in seeing again those we have so dearly loved in this life! Yes, we will even know the new Christians who are now only being converted to our holy faith in the Indies, Japan and the Antipodes. The good friendships of this life will continue eternally in the other. We will love each person with a special love, but these particular friendships will not cause particularity because all of our affections will draw their strength from the charity of God which, ordering all, will make us love each of the blessed with that eternal love with which we are loved by the Divine Majesty.

"Oh God! What consolation we will have in these heavenly conversations with each other. There our good angels will give us greater joy than we can imagine when we recognize them and they speak to us so lovingly of the care they had for our salvation during our mortal life, reminding us of the holy inspirations they gave us, as a sacred milk which they drew from the breast of the Divine Goodness, to attract us to seek the incomparable sweetness we now enjoy. 'Do you remember,' they will say, 'the inspiration I gave you at such a time, in reading that book, or in listening to that sermon, or in looking at that image?'. . . Oh God, will not our hearts melt with indescribable delight in hearing these words?"(*Lenten Sermons*, 58–59).

PRAYER

"When will my soul, Oh Father, be like heaven, lifted above the earth by the force of your love, adorned with as many virtues as the heavens contain astral bodies and stars, firm and strong in your service without every falling just as the heavens do not fall so that it may be all beautiful and pleasing before your face and that you, Father, may deign to dwell there as in a very beautiful heaven?" (*OEA*, 26:396). Amen.

GOSPEL

Jesus took Peter, James and John and led them up a high mountain apart by themselves. And he was transfigured before them, and his clothes became dazzling white, such as no fuller on earth could bleach them. Then Elijah appeared to them along with Moses, and they were conversing with Jesus. Then Peter said to Jesus in reply, "Rabbi, it is good that we are here! Let us make three tents: one for you, one for Moses, and one for Elijah." He hardly knew what to say, they were so terrified. Then a cloud came, casting a shadow over them; from the cloud came a voice, "This is my beloved Son. Listen to him." Suddenly, looking around, they no longer saw anyone but Jesus alone with them.

As they were coming down from the mountain, he charged them not to relate what they had seen to anyone, except when the Son of Man had risen from the dead. So they kept the matter to themselves, questioning what rising from the dead meant.

MARK 9: 2-10

ST. FRANCIS DE SALES

"If you, Father, are in heaven, then it follows that I, your child, am a stranger in this world and that I always walk toward my homeland, which is heaven. If the pilgrim as he walks has his body on the road and his soul in the sweet homeland, every hour seems like a thousand years because of the desire he has to reach it and to see his dear father and brothers. Why wouldn't this be the same for me? Why, our Father, doesn't my soul converse in heaven like the soul of your holy apostle who said: 'Our conversation is heaven' [Phil. 3:20]" (OEA, 26:398).

REFLECTION

"These visions, this gazing, these particular considerations that we will make on this sacred love by which we have been so dearly, so ardently, loved by our sovereign Master, will inflame our hearts with unparalleled ardor and delight. What ought we not do or suffer in order to enjoy these unutterably pleasing delights! This truth is shown in today's Gospel; for do you not see that Moses and Elias spoke and conversed very familiarly indeed with our transfigured Lord? . . . Our felicity will not stop at this . . . It will pass farther, for we will see face to face [1 Cor. 13:12] and very clearly the Divine Majesty, the essence of God, and the mystery of the Most Holy Trinity. In this vision and clear knowledge consists the essence of felicity. There we will understand and participate in those adorable conversations and divine colloquies which take place between the Father, Son and Holy Spirit. We shall listen to how melodiously the Son will intone the praises due to his heavenly Father. . . . In exchange we shall hear the eternal Father, in a thunderous but incomparably harmonious voice, pronounce the divine words which the apostles heard on the day the Transfiguration: 'This is my Beloved Son in whom I am well pleased.' And the Father and the Son, speaking of the Holy Spirit, will say: 'This is Our Spirit, in whom, proceeding one from another, we have placed all Our Love.' . . . Not only will there be conversations between the Divine Persons, but also between God and us. And what will this divine conversation be? Oh, what will it be indeed! It will be such as no man may speak. It will be an intimate conversation so secret that no one will understand it except God and the soul with whom it is made" (*Lenten Sermons*, 62–63).

PRAYER

"You are our Father because you give yourself entirely for us who are so poor and because you have communicated everything to us here below in the Most Holy Sacrament, and then in heaven, you will communicate yourself more clearly, revealing to us your blessed essence, the infinite treasures of your beatitude and the glory of your majesty. So, I beg you, Oh Father, that since you are completely ours, may I also be your child. . . . These words, our Father, will be fitting on my lips when my soul and my body will belong completely to you since you belong completely to us" (*OEA*, 26:395). Amen.

GOSPEL

Jesus took Peter, John, and James and went up the mountain to pray. While he was praying his face changed in appearance and his clothing became dazzling white. And behold, two men were conversing with him, Moses and Elijah, who appeared in glory and spoke of his exodus that he was going to accomplish in Jerusalem. Peter and his companions had been overcome by sleep, but becoming fully awake, they saw his glory and the two men standing with him. As they were about to part from him, Peter said to Jesus, "Master, it is good that we are here; let us make three tents, one for you, one for Moses, and one for Elijah." But he did not know what he was saying. While he was still speaking, a cloud came and cast a shadow over them, and they became frightened when they entered the cloud. Then from the cloud came a voice that said, "This is my chosen Son; listen to him." After the voice had spoken, Jesus was found alone. They fell silent and did not at that time tell anyone what they had seen.

LUKE 9: 28B-36

ST. FRANCIS DE SALES

"Sweetness and consolation are what we persistently desire, but it is the bitter taste of dryness that is profitable. St. Peter would gladly have dwelt upon Mt. Tabor, though he fled from Calvary; but was not the greater work for us done upon the latter? And did not the bloodshed there do more for us than the bright shining light of the former? Francis frequently said: 'It is far better to eat bread without sugar than sugar without bread'" (Camus, 153–54).

REFLECTION

In describing the mystical experience on the Mount of Transfiguration where the exodus from Egypt is alluded to and symbolizes for our saint

85

Jesus' exodus or Passover from this life, he uses the term "excess." The French word *exces* is derived from the Latin *excessus*. This is the word used in the Vulgate edition describing the conversation between Moses and Elias to speak of Jesus' exodus from this life or Passover. Here is the interesting insight that our saint draws: "The apostles saw Moses and Elias speaking to our Lord of the excess which he was to undergo in Jerusalem [Lk. 9:30–31]. During the Transfiguration, the Passion is mentioned, for this excess is nothing other than the Passion. Our divine Master made his excesses in many ways different from ours, for we make ours from below to on high. Excess means ecstasy. So he spoke about his excess. What excess? That God descends from his supreme glory. And for what purpose? To take on our humanity and make it subject to men, indeed even to all human miseries, to the extent that being immortal, he made himself subject to death and to death on the cross [Phil. 2:6–8]. Love does not nourish itself in the manner we think. Our Savior then is talking about his Passion and death because it is the sovereign act of his love. Hence the blessed in eternal glory will speak about nor rejoice in nothing so much as in this death. Consequently, amid consolations, we must remember the Passion. Certainly, we must not say what St. Peter said: 'It is good that we are here,' but 'It is good that we suffer here [below] so as to go to the Mount of Calvary. . . .One heard the voice of the eternal Father which said: 'This is my beloved Son. Listen to him.' We must then obey the eternal Father by following Our Lord in order to hear his word. And this is the way we are instructed, no matter our condition: we must all ask and pray, for it is in prayer that our divine Master principally speaks to us" (*OEA*, 9:28–30).

PRAYER

"I come now, Oh Father, before you with your holy Son, my Lord Jesus Christ. I present him to you and humbly pray that by his merits and his most holy death and Passion, that you deign to grant me what he himself in this prayer and this request which are his and has ordained me to ask you so that my soul may be completely yours and praise and bless you for ever and ever. Amen" (*OEA*, 26:419).

GOSPEL

JESUS SAID TO HIS DISCIPLES:

"Be merciful, just as your Father is merciful.

"Stop judging and you will not be judged. Stop condemning and you will not be condemned. Forgive and you will be forgiven. Give and gifts will be given to you; a good measure, packed together, shaken down, and overflowing, will be poured into your lap. For the measure with which you measure will in return be measured out to you."

LUKE 6: 36-38

ST. FRANCIS DE SALES

"Your mercy is not exhausted since it is infinite. It has not stopped because there are no stopping points and that, furthermore, it would close heaven. It has not ceased because, just as a fire continues to burn as long as it has consumable material, so is your mercy, as long as there are sins to burn and debts to forgive" (OEA, 26:413).

REFLECTION

Our saint tells us, "We do not desire compassion because of the pain it brings our hearts, but rather because such pain unites us and associates us with the one we love who is in pain" (*TLG*, I:250). Therein lies the power of compassion or mercy; it is the power "to be with." For our saint, the perfect exemplar of the virtue of compassion and hence of "being with" is Our Blessed Lady. "She felt the same miseries of her son by commiseration, the same dolors by condolence, and the same passion by compassion" (*TLG*, I:244). The words commiseration, (to share the miseries with), condolence (to share the dolors or sufferings

87

with), and compassion (to suffer with) all emphasize the importance of being with, of being present to, of being there for someone who is suffering and in pain.

Our saint stresses the unifying and transforming power of the love of compassion and makes us better understand its nature. Compassion makes us reach out in love so that we readily identify with those who suffer, and we become like them because love makes us become like the one we love, as he was wont to say (see *IDL*, pt. 3, ch. 15). Mercy or compassion makes us sensitive to what others are suffering and experiencing. The love of compassion gives us the ability to identify with the person we love and makes us appreciate what struggles, difficulties, suffering and hardships others are enduring or can experience, even our enemies. This is why compassionate people are slow to judge and condemn others because they can always make allowances for the pressures and the pain that others might be experiencing. They know what it means to walk a mile in someone else's moccasins, to use a well-known Native American expression.

PRAYER

Merciful and compassionate Father, your presence in the midst of our afflictions is a great source of strength and consolation. Make me realize how important it is to be there for others who are in misery and suffering. Move me to support them in their time of need to help them deal with their difficulties and troubles. Grant this in Jesus' name. Amen.

GOSPEL

Jesus spoke to the crowds and to his disciples, saying, "The scribes and the Pharisees have taken their seat on the chair of Moses. Therefore, do and observe all things whatsoever they tell you, but do not follow their example. For they preach but they do not practice. They tie up heavy burdens hard to carry and lay them on people's shoulders, but they will not lift a finger to move them. All their works are performed to be seen. They widen their phylacteries and lengthen their tassels. They love places of honor at banquets, seats of honor in synagogues, greetings in marketplaces, and the salutation 'Rabbi.' As for you, do not be called 'Rabbi.' You have but one teacher, and you are all brothers. Call no one on earth your father; you have but one Father in heaven. Do not be called 'Master'; you have but one master, the Christ. The greatest among you must be your servant. Whoever exalts himself will be humbled; but whoever humbles himself will be exalted."

MATTHEW 23: 1-12

ST. FRANCIS DE SALES

"We must guard against vanity. Let us listen to the Lord. 'They love the first places at feasts and the first chairs in the synagogues, and salutations in the market place, and to be called by men, Rabbi' [Mt. 23:6–7]. [The scribes and the Pharisees] loved the honor and not the burden [of their positions]. O God!, we must love the sheep for the love of Christ and not out of vanity, not in order to be honored but rather that Christ be honored by them. 'Do you love me? Feed my sheep' [Jn. 21:17]. But with what kind of love? 'To death and death on the cross' [Phil. 2:8].'. . . Nothing is lacking to pastors who love; love itself teaches; it edifies" (OEA, 8:289).

REFLECTION

In the spirit of the prophets of old, our Lord castigates the religious leaders of his day, especially among the Pharisees. We mustn't

89

conclude, however, that all of the Pharisees were religious hypocrites who led people astray by their love of ostentation and their tendency to put the people in a legalistic and ritualistic straight-jacket that is the very antithesis of religion because it never touches people's hearts. There were many good spiritual leaders among the Pharisees of Jesus' day. Jesus was just signaling out a tendency that is prevalent in religious leaders of all times and places. The Pharisees did not have a monopoly on this.

Christ is hitting the human tendency, all too prevalent among religious leaders of whatever era, to be ostentatious and to "pull rank." These people like to broadcast their piety and to bring attention to themselves and to attend social and religious functions seeking some sort of recognition and cheap publicity. Our saint makes the following observation on this gospel passage: "We must guard against vanity. Let us listen to the Lord. [The scribes and the Pharisees] loved the honor and not the burden [of their positions]. O God!, we must love the sheep for the love of Christ and not our of vanity, not in order to be honored but rather that Christ be honored by them. 'Do you love me? Feed my sheep.' [Jn 21:17] But with what kind of love? 'To death and death on the cross'[Phil. 2:8]. . . . Nothing is lacking to pastors who love; love itself teaches; it edifies." We teach and lead primarily by the way we love. By our baptism, we are all called to be religious leaders of one kind or another since we share in the kingship of Jesus. So we must take to heart Jesus' admonition to avoid the tendency of promoting ourselves instead of promoting the Lord.

PRAYER

Lord Jesus, we desperately need to be delivered of the natural tendency to promote and to assert ourselves, especially in our religious practices. During this Lenten season, help us to appreciate the kind of leadership you have given us, a leadership that nourished and supported others by loving and caring for them. May it please you to grant our request. Amen.

GOSPEL

As Jesus was going up to Jerusalem, he took the Twelve disciples aside by themselves, and said to them on the way, "Behold, we are going up to Jerusalem, and the Son of Man will be handed over to the chief priests and the scribes, and they will condemn him to death, and hand him over to the Gentiles to be mocked and scourged and crucified, and he will be raised on the third day."

Then the mother of the sons of Zebedee approached Jesus with her sons and did him homage, wishing to ask him for something. He said to her, "What do you wish?" She answered him, "Command that these two sons of mine sit, one at your right and the other at your left, in your kingdom." Jesus said in reply, "You do not know what you are asking. Can you drink the chalice that I am going to drink?" They said to him, "We can." He replied, "My chalice you will indeed drink, but to sit at my right and at my left, this is not mine to give but is for those for whom it has been prepared by my Father." When the ten heard this, they became indignant at the two brothers. But Jesus summoned them and said, "You know that the rulers of the Gentiles lord it over them, and the great ones make their authority over them felt. But it shall not be so among you. Rather, whoever wishes to be great among you shall be your servant; whoever wishes to be first among you shall be your slave. Just so, the Son of Man did not come to be served but to serve and to give his life as a ransom for many."

MATTHEW 20: 17-28

ST. FRANCIS DE SALES

"We do not understand any of these things, or if we do it is only a superficial knowledge, one that does not reach the inner recesses of our hearts. We are like those who understand without understanding. We do not understand what we do not want to understand. We look for diversions" (OEA, 8:293).

REFLECTION

Our saint found the brazen request of the Mother of James and John to be completely out of place. While the Lord was trying to make his disciples understand that he was going up to Jerusalem not to claim political power but to suffer an ignominious death, their mother along with her sons are preoccupied with honors and preferment. It struck for him, as it should for us, a discordant chord that betrayed a selfish ambition which blinds us to the true nature and mission of the Messiah. Early on, the disciples did not seem to understand how inseparable the cross is from Jesus and his mission. Time and time again, Jesus attempted to get this across to them, and they just didn't get it for a long time. Our saint found consolation in this because he believed it gave us hope. Like them, we might be reluctant to associate suffering and the cross with our Savior and our God. So if it took some doing on Jesus' part to make them understand that he came to serve, suffer and die and that all of his followers must in many ways tread the same path, there is hope for us. Suffering naturally suggests to us something unpleasant and to be avoided at all costs. This attitude interferes with our coming to understand what the cost of discipleship is—that we must all drink of the cup that Jesus drank. Our saint has the following insight on our lack of comprehension: "We do not understand anything [about Jesus crucified], or if we do have some understanding, it is only on the surface and not in the depths of our heart. We are like those who understand without understanding. We do not understand that which we do not want to understand. We look for diversions" (*OEA*, 8:293). As we ponder this scriptural passage during this Lenten season, we ask the Lord to give us the light to understand how to accept and join our sufferings to his.

PRAYER

Lord, I say with the psalmist, "I will take the cup of life; I will call God's name all my days" [Ps. 116]. In this way, may my understanding of your suffering and death resonate in the depth of my heart and lead me to give generously of myself to others. Grant this in Jesus' name. Amen.

GOSPEL

JESUS SAID TO THE PHARISEES:

"There was a rich man who dressed in purple garments and fine linen and dined sumptuously each day. And lying at his door was a poor man named Lazarus, covered with sores, who would gladly have eaten his fill of the scraps that fell from the rich man's table. Dogs even used to come and lick his sores. When the poor man died, he was carried away by angels to the bosom of Abraham. The rich man also died and was buried, and from the netherworld, where he was in torment, he raised his eyes and saw Abraham far off and Lazarus at his side. And he cried out, 'Father Abraham, have pity on me. Send Lazarus to dip the tip of his finger in water and cool my tongue, for I am suffering torment in these flames.' Abraham replied, 'My child, remember that you received what was good during your lifetime while Lazarus likewise received what was bad; but now he is comforted here, whereas you are tormented. Moreover, between us and you a great chasm is established to prevent anyone from crossing who might wish to go from our side to yours or from your side to ours.' He said, 'Then I beg you, father, send him to my father's house, for I have five brothers, so that he may warn them, lest they too come to this place of torment.' But Abraham replied, 'They have Moses and the prophets. Let them listen to them.' He said, 'Oh no, father Abraham, but if someone from the dead goes to them, they will repent.' Then Abraham said, 'If they will not listen to Moses and the prophets, neither will they be persuaded if someone should rise from the dead.'"

LUKE 16: 19-31

ST. FRANCIS DE SALES

"Love the poor and love poverty, for it is by such love that you become truly poor. As the Scripture says, we become like the things we love [Hosea 9:10]. Love makes lovers equal . . . If you love the poor, be often with them. Be glad to see them in your home and to visit them in theirs. Be pleased to talk to them and be pleased to have them near you in church" (IDL, pt. 3, ch. 15).

REFLECTION

Many who have a good supply of material resources suffer from a poverty of awareness, an affliction that can be just as devastating and demoralizing as material poverty. The parable of Lazarus and the Rich Man is intended to make us all conscious of our poverty of awareness which makes so many of us insensitive and unfeeling toward the suffering and misery of others. It helps us to enrich our capacity for compassion. How many times did the rich man pass by the miserable Lazarus with the dog licking his sores and never really notice him? He was too wrapped up in himself and in his own pursuits to think about the misery and suffering of someone who was at his own doorstep, someone whom he literally had to trip over to get into his own house. Every time the rich man walked pass Lazarus he was building his own hell; and every time that Lazarus refused to be embittered by the indifference and insensitivity of others and "by the bitter bread of poverty, he was building a home in heaven."[1] The parable does not tell us that the rich man was evil nor intentionally cruel but rather too concerned with himself and his own pursuits. He just never bothered himself about Lazarus. In all likelihood, the rich man not only gave Lazarus scraps from his table but alms to the poor. But he did not make himself

---

1. George Buttrick, "The Gospel According to Luke," in *The Interpreter's Bible,* New York: Abingdon Press, 1952, vol. VIII, 290.

aware of Lazarus. He did not say: "This man is wallowing in misery and longs for God. He doesn't know where his next meal is coming from. He keeps asking himself: 'Why does this have to happen to me.?'" And so he passed him by without a second thought.

Our Lord's solution for dealing with this poverty of awareness is to listen to "Moses and the prophets," that is, to Sacred Scripture and especially to this powerful parable. Following Jesus' admonition, our saint tells us to love the poor by being with them and serving them. In this way, we become like those we love and begin to build our heaven on earth by overcoming our poverty of awareness.

PRAYER

Lord, help me to sharpen my vision and be more sensitive to the needs of the less fortunate with whom I come in contact. Give me that compassionate love that so characterized your life and teaching so that I may joyfully reach out to alleviate the needs of others who are struggling to make ends meet. I ask this through Jesus Christ, your Son. Amen.

GOSPEL

JESUS SAID TO THE CHIEF PRIESTS AND
THE ELDERS OF THE PEOPLE:

"Hear another parable. There was a landowner who planted a vineyard, put a hedge around it, dug a wine press in it, and built a tower. Then he leased it to tenants and went on a journey. When vintage time drew near, he sent his servants to the tenants to obtain his produce. But the tenants seized the servants and one they beat, another they killed, and a third they stoned. Again he sent other servants, more numerous than the first ones, but they treated them in the same way. Finally, he sent his son to them, thinking, 'They will respect my son.' But when the tenants saw the son, they said to one another, 'This is the heir. Come, let us kill him and acquire his inheritance.' They seized him, threw him out of the vineyard, and killed him. What will the owner of the vineyard do to those tenants when he comes?" They answered him, "He will put those wretched men to a wretched death and lease his vineyard to other tenants who will give him the produce at the proper times." Jesus said to them, "Did you never read in the Scriptures:

The stone that the builders rejected
has become the cornerstone;
by the Lord has this been done,
and it is wonderful in our eyes?

Therefore, I say to you, the Kingdom of God will be taken away from you and given to a people that will produce its fruit."

When the chief priests and the Pharisees heard his parables, they knew that he was speaking about them. And although they were attempting to arrest him, they feared the crowds, for they regarded him as a prophet.

MATTHEW 21: 33-43, 45-46

ST. FRANCIS DE SALES

"[Our] souls are God's vineyard" (OEA, 13:145).

REFLECTION

In an early letter to St. Jane de Chantal, our saint gives an intriguing allegorical interpretation of this parable. He tells her that in a sermon he is going to compare our souls to God's vine, the cistern to faith, the tower to hope, and the wine press to holy charity, and the hedge to God's law. However, he personalizes this parable for her and says, "Your good will is your vineyard; the cistern are the inspirations of perfection that God causes to rain down there from the sky. The tower is holy chastity, which . . . must be of ivory. The wine press is obedience, which results in great merit by those actions in which it is carried out. The hedges are your vows. Oh! God preserve this vine which your hand has planted. God desires that the salutary waters of his graces keep increasing in this cistern. May God always be the protector of this tower" (*OEA*, 13:145).

In personalizing the parable in this fashion, our saint gives an immediacy and intimacy to it which makes us realize how close God is to us and how diligently we must cultivate this vine, especially during Lent, so as to bring forth the fruit of the vine that God expects from us when he sends his messengers, that is, his inspirations. We must not reject them for to do so would bring great destruction to our spiritual lives, but we must give them a warm and gracious welcome. Grapes, the fruit of the vine produce wine, which Sacred Scripture tells us that God has created to bring joy to our hearts. As one wag has remarked: "Wine doth gladden the heart of man, and doth not sadden the heart of women." So as God's vine, we can readily see that we must produce the wine of gladness by the way we live in order to bring joy to the hearts of others. Our saint gives a rather unusual and upbeat interpretation or understanding of this parable.

PRAYER

Father, your servant Francis de Sales urges us to "Live joyfully and be generous; that is what [You], whom we love and to whom we are dedicated, want us to be." May this joy we experience overflow into the lives of those who cross our path.[1] We ask this in Jesus' name. Amen.

---

1. See *Francis De Sales: Selected Letters,* trans. Elizabeth Stopp (New York: Harper, 1960), 97–98.

GOSPEL

Tax collectors and sinners were all drawing near to listen to Jesus, but the Pharisees and scribes began to complain, saying, "This man welcomes sinners and eats with them." So to them Jesus addressed this parable. "A man had two sons, and the younger son said to his father, 'Father, give me the share of your estate that should come to me.' So the father divided the property between them. After a few days, the younger son collected all his belongings and set off to a distant country where he squandered his inheritance on a life of dissipation. When he had freely spent everything, a severe famine struck that country, and he found himself in dire need. So he hired himself out to one of the local citizens who sent him to his farm to tend the swine. And he longed to eat his fill of the pods on which the swine fed, but nobody gave him any. Coming to his senses he thought, 'How many of my father's hired workers have more than enough food to eat, but here am I, dying from hunger. I shall get up and go to my father and I shall say to him, "Father, I have sinned against heaven and against you. I no longer deserve to be called your son; treat me as you would treat one of your hired workers."' So he got up and went back to his father. While he was still a long way off, his father caught sight of him, and was filled with compassion. He ran to his son, embraced him and kissed him. His son said to him, 'Father, I have sinned against heaven and against you; I no longer deserve to be called your son.' But his father ordered his servants, 'Quickly, bring the finest robe and put it on him; put a ring on his finger and sandals on his feet. Take the fattened calf and slaughter it. Then let us celebrate with a feast, because this son of mine was dead, and has come to life again; he was lost, and has been found.' Then the celebration began. Now the older son had been out in the field and, on his way back, as he neared the house, he heard the sound of music and dancing. He called one of the servants and asked what this might mean. The servant said to him, 'Your brother has returned and your father has slaughtered the fattened calf because he has him back safe and sound.' He became angry, and when he refused to enter the house, his father came out and pleaded with him. He said to his father in reply, 'Look, all these years I served you and not once did I disobey your orders; yet you never gave me even a young goat to feast on with my friends. But when your son returns who swallowed up your property with prostitutes, for him you slaughter the fattened calf.' He said to him, 'My son, you are here with me always; everything I have is yours. But now we must celebrate and rejoice, because your brother was dead and has come to life again; he was lost and has been found.'"

LUKE 15: 1-3, 11-32

ST. FRANCIS DE SALES

"I always say that our misery is the throne of God's mercy, and so we must realize that the greater our misery, the greater should be our confidence in [God]" (OEA, 6:22).

REFLECTION

"I am mindful, Oh Father, of the compassion you showed to your ancient people whose sins you forgave so many times. I recall, Oh Father, that you remembered your servant David and that you forgave his grave sin. [2 Sam. 12:13]. I remember, Oh Father, that your well-beloved Son, while on this earth, looked with mercy on his apostle when he denied him [Lk. 22:55–61] and Mary Magdalene when she repented [Lk. 7:37–50] and finally that he received all repentant sinners and ate with them [Lk. 15:1–2]. You have not changed; you were once a very merciful God; you are not less so now; you are the same God as before. Your mercy is not exhausted since it is infinite. It has not stopped because there are no stopping points and that, furthermore, it would close heaven. It has not ceased because, just as a fire continues to burn as long as it has consumable material, so is your mercy, as long as there are sins to burn and debts to forgive. 'His mercy extends from age to age on those who fear him,' the canticle of the Most holy Mother of your blessed Son, our Lord Jesus Christ, who knows full well that it is immense [Lk 1:50]. You have set limits to the extent of the sea, but you have not set any limits to your mercy so that it always goes in search of sinners overburdened with debts to pardon them. Your mercy, Oh Father, goes out to encounter the greatest sinner of them all, the one who has more debts than any other child of Adam. Wipe out my sins; forgive me the great sum of my debts and always press on to find other debtors. 'Deep calls unto deep' [Ps. 42:8]. The miserable son calls out to the Father of mercies. May deep absorb another deep; may the depth of my infinite miseries be absorbed by the depth [of your mercy]" (*OEA*, 26:414).

PRAYER

"This word, 'Father,' encourages me so that when I fall, I may run to throw myself contritely into your arms, for I will be received more lovingly than the Prodigal son. And now, remembering my past faults, I run toward you, Father, and I say: 'Father, I have sinned against heaven and you; I am not worthy to be called your son; treat me like one of your hired hands'" (*OEA*, 26:392). Amen.

QUESTIONS FOR REFLECTION
OR DISCUSSION

1. What image of compassion do you find touches you the most and why?

2. What is the image of Jesus that is uppermost in your mind and why? How does this square with the image that Jesus has of himself?

3. In your religious practices, do you have a tendency of wanting to impress others? If so, how do you deal with this tendency?

4. With whom do you identify in the parable of the Prodigal Son and why?

THIRD WEEK
OF
LENT

GOSPEL

Jesus came to a town of Samaria called Sychar, near the plot of land that Jacob had given to his son Joseph. Jacob's well was there. Jesus, tired from his journey, sat down there at the well. It was about noon.

A woman of Samaria came to draw water. Jesus said to her, "Give me a drink." His disciples had gone into the town to buy food. The Samaritan woman said to him, "How can you, a Jew, ask me, a Samaritan woman, for a drink?" — For Jews use nothing in common with Samaritans. — Jesus answered and said to her, "If you knew the gift of God and who is saying to you, 'Give me a drink,' you would have asked him and he would have given you living water." The woman said to him, "Sir, you do not even have a bucket and the cistern is deep; where then can you get this living water? Are you greater than our father Jacob, who gave us this cistern and drank from it himself with his children and his flocks?" Jesus answered and said to her, "Everyone who drinks this water will be thirsty again; but whoever drinks the water I shall give will never thirst; the water I shall give will become in him a spring of water welling up to eternal life." The woman said to him, "Sir, give me this water, so that I may not be thirsty or have to keep coming here to draw water."

Jesus said to her, "Go call your husband and come back." The woman answered and said to him, "I do not have a husband." Jesus answered her, "You are right in saying, 'I do not have a husband.' For you have had five husbands, and the one you have now is not your husband. What you have said is true." The woman said to him, "Sir, I can see that you are a prophet. Our ancestors worshiped on this mountain; but you people say that the place to worship is in Jerusalem." Jesus said to her, "Believe me, woman, the hour is coming when you will worship the Father neither on this mountain nor in Jerusalem. You people worship what you do not understand; we worship what we understand, because salvation is from the Jews. But the hour is coming, and is now here, when true worshipers will worship the Father in Spirit and truth; and indeed the

Father seeks such people to worship him. God is Spirit, and those who worship him must worship in Spirit and truth." The woman said to him, "I know that the Messiah is coming, the one called the Christ; when he comes, he will tell us everything." Jesus said to her, "I am he, the one speaking with you."

At that moment his disciples returned, and were amazed that he was talking with a woman, but still no one said, "What are you looking for?" or "Why are you talking with her?" The woman left her water jar and went into the town and said to the people, "Come see a man who told me everything I have done. Could he possibly be the Christ?" They went out of the town and came to him. Meanwhile, the disciples urged him, "Rabbi, eat." But he said to them, "I have food to eat of which you do not know." So the disciples said to one another, "Could someone have brought him something to eat?" Jesus said to them, "My food is to do the will of the one who sent me and to finish his work. Do you not say, 'In four months the harvest will be here'? I tell you, look up and see the fields ripe for the harvest. The reaper is already receiving payment and gathering crops for eternal life, so that the sower and reaper can rejoice together. For here the saying is verified that 'One sows and another reaps.' I sent you to reap what you have not worked for; others have done the work, and you are sharing the fruits of their work."

Many of the Samaritans of that town began to believe in him because of the word of the woman who testified, "He told me everything I have done." When the Samaritans came to him, they invited him to stay with them; and he stayed there two days. Many more began to believe in him because of his word, and they said to the woman, "We no longer believe because of your word; for we have heard for ourselves, and we know that this is truly the savior of the world."

JOHN 4: 5-42

Shorter form: JOHN 4:5-15, 19b-26, 39a, 40-42
Longer form may be optionally read on any day in the third week of Lent

ST. FRANCIS DE SALES

"So loving is God's hand as it handles our hearts! So skillful is it in bringing its strength to us without depriving us of freedom, and in imparting to us the movement resulting from its power without hindering the movement of our will" (TLG, I: 133).

REFLECTION

Chance encounters often have consequences that change our lives. Of course, our saint firmly believed that nothing every really happens by chance but that everything is ordered in some mysterious and marvelous way by God's loving providence. This is certainly evident in the encounter that the Samaritan woman had with Jesus. It was life-changing for her and for a number of other people. Jesus scandalized people of his day by breaking religious and social taboos, but not for the sake of breaking them. Jews did not talk to Samaritans because of very bitter religious differences alluded to in his conversation with the Samaritan woman. Furthermore, men never spoke to women in public not even their own wives! Jesus simply ignored these artificial barriers erected by our religious and cultural hang-ups that keep people alienated and separated from one another. He meets the woman on a very human level—as another human being who needs him. That's all he is concerned about. Remember. In the eyes of the Jews, the Samaritan woman was the lowest of the low. This is why she is so surprised to see Jesus speak to her, and she replies, "You are a Jew. How can you ask me, a Samaritan and a woman, for a drink?"

Jesus is very human here. He is tired, hungry and thirsty. He uses the occasion of his own needs and those of others to make contact with people and bring them the good news of salvation. That's the way he ordinarily comes into our lives—in a very casual and unsuspecting fashion—a relative in need, a neighbor who has some serious family problems and brings them to us over a cup of coffee or a glass of beer.

We can find Jesus in the most ordinary occurrences of our lives.

Jesus does not get bogged down by side issues. When Jesus says that he can give her water that will relieve her thirst forever, she objects and says, "You don't have a bucket, and this well is deep. Where do you expect to get this flowing water? She protests that he can't be greater than the patriarch Jacob. Jesus lifts her mind to spiritual things. He avoids theological disputes on different places of worship and goes to what is essential. The place is not what is important but our interior disposition. God seeks people who will worship him in spirit and in truth, that is, with heart and mind in the right place. The woman never expected that kind of an answer after having heard the quibbling distinctions made by her religious leaders.

The woman is won over completely. She asks for this living water that Jesus can give, and she begins to understand the gift of God, although she still looked on this living water in a physical way. ("So I don't have to come here and get water.") This gift of living water is the gift of the Holy Spirit as Christ himself states in the seventh chapter of this Gospel. Jesus struck the rock of her heart so that the living water of God's love would flow out and others could drink from it. She rushes back to tell of her experience with Jesus. It was just too good to keep to herself (the first evangelist?). So she wanted others to come to know Jesus as she had. An authentic experience and contact with Christ moves us to share it with others. It's just too good to keep to ourselves. It makes us all evangelists.

The townspeople accepted the woman's testimony despite the way it happened to her. Because of what she said, they went out to see for themselves. They were not satisfied with getting it second-hand. Once they did come in contact with Christ, they no longer believed in the woman's say-so but in Christ's say-so. "As they told the woman, 'No longer does our faith depend on your story. We have heard for our-selves, and we know that this really is the Savior of the world." Mature faith demands this.

There are many important points that we can learn from this gospel passage: 1) We see how Jesus uses the most unlikely people to reach out and save others in the most ordinary circumstances of our lives; 2) This one individual, a woman, became a fountain bearing the living water to many other people by sharing her intimate experience with others; 3) It highlights the importance of women in spreading the good news and bringing others to faith; and, 4) Our faith will only be solid and mature if its based on direct, immediate and personal contact with Christ and his word.

PRAYER

We know and firmly believe, Lord, that nothing happens to us by chance. Your loving and guiding providence makes us realize how you are working in our lives and in the lives of others in the most ordinary and unspectacular circumstances. May we grow in this realization and come to understand how precious all of these moments are for time and eternity. We ask this in Jesus' name. Amen.

GOSPEL

Since the Passover of the Jews was near, Jesus went up to Jerusalem. He found in the temple area those who sold oxen, sheep and doves, as well as the money changers seated there. He made a whip out of cords and drove them all out of the temple area, with sheep and oxen, and spilled the coins of the money changers and overturned their tables, and to those who sold doves he said, "Take these out of here, and stop making my Father's house a marketplace." His disciples recalled the words of Scripture, *Zeal for your house will consume me.* At this the Jews answered and said to him, "What sign can you show us for doing this?" Jesus answered and said to them, "Destroy this temple and in three days I will raise it up." The Jews said, "This temple has been under construction for forty-six years, and you will raise it up in three days?" But he was speaking about the temple of his body. Therefore, when he was raised from the dead, his disciples remembered that he had said this, and they came to believe the Scripture and the word Jesus had spoken.

While he was in Jerusalem for the feast of Passover, many began to believe in his name when they saw the signs he was doing. But Jesus would not trust himself to them because he knew them all, and did not need anyone to testify about human nature. He himself understood it well.

JOHN 2: 13-25

ST. FRANCIS DE SALES

"Since zeal is ardent, vehement love, it requires prudent direction; otherwise, it would exceed the bounds of moderation and discretion" (TLG, II:181).

REFLECTION

"We can be zealous in three ways. First by carrying out great acts of justice to repel evil. This belongs only to those who in their character as superiors, such as magistrates, prelates, and preachers have the public duty to correct, censure, and reprimand others. But because this office is one of honor, everyone takes it upon himself to have part in it. Secondly, we can be zealous by doing acts of great virtue in order to give good example by suggesting remedies for evil, exhorting men to apply them, and doing the good opposed to the evil we wish to eradicate. This holds for all of us, but few men wish to do so. Finally, the most excellent exercise of zeal consists in suffering and enduring many things in order to prevent or avert evil. Almost no one wants to exercise this kind of zeal. A show of zeal is our whole ambition. It is on this that each of us wishes to employ his talents, without seeing that it is not zeal that we look for but glory and the satisfaction of arrogance, anger, pique, and other passions.

"'Happy the man who knows how to control zeal,' says St. Ambrose, and St. Bernard says, 'The devil will easily delude your zeal, if you neglect knowledge. Therefore, let you zeal be inflamed with charity, adorned with knowledge, and established in constancy.' True zeal is the child of charity, since it is its ardor. Therefore, like charity, it is patient, kind, without trouble, without quarreling, without hatred, without envy, and it rejoices in the truth. The ardor of true zeal is like the hunter's; it is diligent, careful, active, industrious, eager in pursuit, but without passion, anger or disquiet, for if the hunter's work were done in anger, bad temper, and vexation, it would not be liked and desired so much. In like manner, zeal has ardors that are extreme but stable, solid, [gentle], industrious, and equally agreeable and untiring. Completely different is false zeal: it is turbulent, troubled, insolent, arrogant, choleric, quick to pass, and in equal measure impetuous and unstable" (*TLG*, II:189–90).

PRAYER

Strengthen and deepen our love for you, Lord, so that we may be zealous in serving you. Yet, make us mindful of how dangerous zeal can be when it becomes the vehicle of giving free rein to our passions and our selfish ambition and thereby becoming destructive of the good we desire to accomplish. May our zeal be solely motivated to please you. We ask this in Jesus' name. Amen.

GOSPEL

Some people told Jesus about the Galileans whose blood Pilate had mingled with the blood of their sacrifices. Jesus said to them in reply, "Do you think that because these Galileans suffered in this way they were greater sinners than all other Galileans? By no means! But I tell you, if you do not repent, you will all perish as they did! Or those eighteen people who were killed when the tower at Siloam fell on them – do you think they were more guilty than everyone else who lived in Jerusalem? By no means! But I tell you, if you do not repent, you will all perish as they did!"

And he told them this parable: "There once was a person who had a fig tree planted in his orchard, and when he came in search of fruit on it but found none, he said to the gardener, 'For three years now I have come in search of fruit on this fig tree but have found none. So cut it down. Why should it exhaust the soil?' He said to him in reply, 'Sir, leave it for this year also, and I shall cultivate the ground around it and fertilize it; it may bear fruit in the future. If not you can cut it down.'"

LUKE 13: 1-9

ST. FRANCIS DE SALES

"[God] has promised forgiveness to the repentant, but he has not promised to give us the time to repent" (OEA, 7:128).

REFLECTION

Jesus' hearers believed that physical evil, pain and suffering were to be seen as a punishment from God and a sign of his displeasure. This is evident from the two incidents cited in today's Gospel. The first is an allusion to a massacre ordered by Pilate in the very precincts of the temple when certain Jews were preparing their sacrifices as sin offerings. This is the meaning of the allusion to the "Galileans whose blood Pilate had mixed with their sacrifices." They were implicitly asking Jesus, "How could they be punished by God in this way when they were in the very act of offering sacrifice and worship to God?" Of course, Jesus answered by saying that this was not necessarily an indication of God's displeasure with them, or that he was more displeased with them than he was with other people of that time. He gave a similar answer for the people who were killed when a tower collapsed on them. This was not a sign that God's punishment was being visited upon them because of their great sinfulness. The point that Jesus is making is simply this: "Just because you may be doing well and prospering both in material things and in your health, you should not mistakenly conclude that everything is right between you and God and that these good things are a sign of God's blessings on you and your family and loved ones." St. Paul tells us that God's patience is intended to lead us to repentance (see Rom. 2:4–5). Jesus is asking and warning us to take to heart his call to reform our lives, to turn our lives around during this season of Lent and to give them a new direction so that a far worse fate than physical evils will not be our lot.

PRAYER

Merciful Father, make us aware that the time for us to repent of our waywardness is not limitless. Give us a sense of urgency and the grace to seize the present moment to make things right between us so that our repentance may give joy to your heart and free us to commit ourselves completely to your service. Grant this in the name of Jesus, your Son. Amen.

GOSPEL

JESUS SAID TO THE PEOPLE IN THE SYNAGOGUE
AT NAZARETH:

"Amen, I say to you, no prophet is accepted in his own native place.
Indeed, I tell you, there were many widows in Israel in the days of Elijah
when the sky was closed for three and a half years and a severe famine
spread over the entire land. It was to none of these that Elijah was sent,
but only to a widow in Zarephath in the land of Sidon. Again, there
were many lepers in Israel during the time of Elisha the prophet; yet
not one of them was cleansed, but only Naaman the Syrian." When
the people in the synagogue heard this, they were all filled with fury.
They rose up, drove him out of the town, and led him to the brow of
the hill on which their town had been built, to hurl him down head-
long. But he passed through the midst of them and went away.

LUKE 4: 24-30

ST. FRANCIS DE SALES

*"When God desires to give us his graces, it is pride to refuse them . . .
God's gifts obligate us to accept them, and . . . it is humility to obey and
comply as nearly as we can with his desires? It is God's will"* (IDL, pt.
3, ch. 5).

REFLECTION

The bible history lesson that Jesus gives his hometown folks is met
with great indignation and resentment. They see Jesus as describing a
God quite different from the one they know, one who reaches out to

foreigners and even to those who oppressed them and seems to favor these people over them, God's chosen people. Another point that Jesus wants to make is the importance of so-called "nobodies" in God's plan for salvation. He tells them that God writes history differently than we do. We write it primarily from the viewpoint of the lives and actions of those who are rich and wield power – rulers, kings, generals, legislators, celebrities. We see in the story of Naaman the Syrian, a powerful general, that it is the powerless, the little and supposedly insignificant people, the "nobodies" that make things happen, who are the real protagonists of the story. It is the servant girl of Naaman's wife who suggests to her mistress that the Syrian general go to Samaria and ask the prophet Elisha to cure him. When his pride gets the best of him and he is insulted when told to bathe seven times in the muddy waters of the Jordan, it is his servants who urge him to follow the prophet's advice. So we see that these "nobodies," these little people not only play an essential role in bringing him a cure, but also and more importantly help to bring him to faith in the one true God as a result of their actions.

PRAYER

There are times, Lord, when we feel like we are a "nobody" and that we really don't matter to you or count for anything. At those times, let us not get down on ourselves but rather be encouraged by how you use the many small, little and insignificant people to accomplish your will. Make us receptive to playing the role you have designated for us in your plan of salvation. We ask this in Jesus' name. Amen.

GOSPEL

Peter approached Jesus and asked him, "Lord, if my brother sins against me, how often must I forgive him? As many as seven times?" Jesus answered, "I say to you, not seven times but seventy-seven times. That is why the Kingdom of heaven may be likened to a king who decided to settle accounts with his servants. When he began the accounting, a debtor was brought before him who owed him a huge amount. Since he had no way of paying it back, his master ordered him to be sold, along with his wife, his children, and all his property, in payment of the debt. At that, the servant fell down, did him homage, and said, 'Be patient with me, and I will pay you back in full.' Moved with compassion the master of that servant let him go and forgave him the loan. When that servant had left, he found one of his fellow servants who owed him a much smaller amount. He seized him and started to choke him, demanding, 'Pay back what you owe.' Falling to his knees, his fellow servant begged him, 'Be patient with me, and I will pay you back.' But he refused. Instead, he had him put in prison until he paid back the debt. Now when his fellow servants saw what had happened, they were deeply disturbed, and went to their master and reported the whole affair. His master summoned him and said to him, 'You wicked servant! I forgave you your entire debt because you begged me to. Should you not have had pity on your fellow servant, as I had pity on you?' Then in anger his master handed him over to the torturers until he should pay back the whole debt. So will my heavenly Father do to you, unless each of you forgives your brother from your heart."

MATTHEW 18: 21-35

ST. FRANCIS DE SALES

"Forgive me the debt of so many sins by which I have offended you: 'Oh God, whose nature it is to be always merciful and to pardon,' have mercy on this poor child and forgive me all my debts" (OEA, 26:412).

REFLECTION

Our saint was very much aware how we humans find it so difficult to forgive, that forgiveness does not come easy to us and that we would like to put a limit on it. To encourage and motivate us, he makes this reflection on how Jesus forgives us: "'My Father, forgive them because they do not know what they are doing' [Lk. 23:34]. What an incomparable statement of perfect love! 'Love one another as I have loved you' [Jn. 13:34], he often said while preaching to the people or to his apostles in such a way that he did not seem to have any affection for any other thing than to inculcate this very holy love. But here he gives us an unimaginable example. He forgives the very ones who are crucifying him and abusing him in a barbaric rage and seeks to find excuses so that his Father may forgive them, and he does this in their very act of sin and abuse. Oh, how wretched we others are, for we can scarcely forget an injury ten years after it has happened. Yes, it even occurs at the hour of death that people cannot even hear the name spoken of those who have done them some wrong and do not want to pardon them. Oh, God how great is our wretchedness! We can scarcely forgive our enemies and Our Lord loved them so dearly and prayed ardently for them!" (*OEA*, 9:272).

PRAYER

Father, help us to understand and appreciate the liberating power of forgiveness. As one writer has aptly stated, "Forgiveness frees the forgiver."[1] Give us merciful, compassionate and forgiving hearts that free us to express our love for you and for our weak and vulnerable brothers and sisters. Grant this through Christ Our Lord. Amen.

---

3. Lance Morrow, *TIME*, Jan. 8, 1984.

GOSPEL

JESUS SAID TO HIS DISCIPLES:

"Do not think that I have come to abolish the law or the prophets. I have come not to abolish but to fulfill. Amen, I say to you, until heaven and earth pass away, not the smallest letter or the smallest part of a letter will pass from the law, until all things have taken place. Therefore, whoever breaks one of the least of these commandments and teaches others to do so will be called least in the Kingdom of heaven. But whoever obeys and teaches these commandments will be called greatest in the Kingdom of heaven."

MATTHEW 5: 17-19

ST. FRANCIS DE SALES

"Do all through love and nothing through constraint. Love obedience more than you fear disobedience" (OEA, 12:359).

REFLECTION

A number of years ago, Ted Koppel of "Nightline" fame, stated in a commencement address that God's commands are not the "Ten Suggestions" but the "Ten Commandments." Unfortunately, many who accept them as commandments rather than mere suggestions look upon them primarily as life-constricting. Pope John Paul II knew how to present them not as life-constricting but as life-giving and love-giving. This is the way he reflected on them during his pilgrimage to Mt. Sinai: "Thus 'the Ten Commandments are the law of freedom . . . *the freedom to love, to choose what is good in every situation.* . . . The Ten Commandments *'stand at the very heart of the truth about man and his destiny.'*[1] To be faithful to the Ten Commandments, to be faithful to God who wrote them in our hearts and on the tablets of the law, "is being faithful to ourselves, to our true nature, and to our deepest and irrepressible aspirations."[2] This captures what Jesus means when he says he has come not to abolish the law and the prophets but to fulfill them. As Moses insists, God's commands are an expression and a manifestation of God's closeness to us and of his merciful love for us. By observing them, we manifest our love for God and for one another. This is certainly the emphasis that Jesus gives to God's commandments in John's Gospel. There we read, "Whoever has my commandments and observes them is the one who loves me. And whoever loves me will be loved by my Father, and I will love him and reveal myself to him" (Jn. 14:21).

Our saint, following St. Paul, believed that love is the fulfillment of the law, and he has captured the essential attitude that we must have toward God's will as known through the Torah and the prophets when he says: "Do all through love and nothing through constraint. Love obedience more than you fear disobedience" *(OEA, 12:359).* So by observing God's law not by constraint but out of love, we get a more profound understanding of Jesus and of ourselves. This is why Scripture speaks of God's law as more precious than gold.

PRAYER

God, give me the joy of knowing and following your law. May I discern your will for me to walk in newness of life. We make our prayer through Christ our Lord. Amen.

---

1. Pope John Paul II, *Blessed are the Pure of Heart* (229), in George Weigel, *The Truth of Catholicism,* 82–83.
2. Pope John Paul II (241–46), in ibid.

GOSPEL

Jesus was driving out a demon that was mute, and when the demon had gone out, the mute man spoke and the crowds were amazed. Some of them said, "By the power of Beelzebul, the prince of demons, he drives out demons." Others, to test him, asked him for a sign from heaven. But he knew their thoughts and said to them, "Every kingdom divided against itself will be laid waste and house will fall against house. And if Satan is divided against himself, how will his kingdom stand? For you say that it is by Beelzebul that I drive out demons. If I, then, drive out demons by Beelzebul, by whom do your own people drive them out? Therefore they will be your judges. But if it is by the finger of God that I drive out demons, then the Kingdom of God has come upon you. When a strong man fully armed guards his palace, his possessions are safe. But when one stronger than he attacks and overcomes him, he takes away the armor on which he relied and distributes the spoils. Whoever is not with me is against me, and whoever does not gather with me scatters."

LUKE 11: 14-23

ST. FRANCIS DE SALES

"Experience has taught us . . . that the naturally weakened mind of man is more inclined to seize upon an objection than on the answer which meets it" (Camus, 201).

REFLECTION

This passage calls to mind the saying: "There is none so blind that will not see and none so deaf that will not hear." When reality collides with our view of God, the world, and ourselves, we have a tendency of either denying the reality, or misconstruing and distorting it. This Gospel passage clearly shows how the reality and truth of Jesus' life and teaching collides with those of closed minds and hearts. When such people are confronted with the absurdity of their position, they dig in their heels and become obstinate by either denying what is under their very noses or ask for further proof, additional signs to put off or avoid acknowledging the truth of what they witness. Jesus' listeners witnessed his dispelling a demon and yet remained in denial or asked for what they supposed was a more convincing sign. But Jesus keeps driving his point home and makes it crystal clear that they are experiencing the benevolent and merciful action of God in their midst and that they have sufficient evidence of the truth that he is performing all of his works through the very power of God that resides in him. To acknowledge this truth is to be with him and to deny it is to be against him.

PRAYER

We want to be with you, Lord, all the way. Give us supple minds and hearts that make us totally receptive to your working in our lives and in our world in so many beautiful and endearing ways. May this truth shape our thinking and our lives. We ask this through Christ Our Lord. Amen.

GOSPEL

One of the scribes came to Jesus and asked him, "Which is the first of all the commandments?" Jesus replied, "The first is this: *Hear, O Israel! The Lord our God is Lord alone! You shall love the Lord your God with all your heart, with all your soul, with all your mind, and with all your strength.* The second is this: *You shall love your neighbor as yourself.* There is no other commandment greater than these." The scribe said to him, "Well said, teacher. You are right in saying, *He is One and there is no other than he.* And *to love him with all your heart, with all your understanding, with all your strength, and to love your neighbor as yourself* is worth more than all burnt offerings and sacrifices." And when Jesus saw that he answered with understanding, he said to him, "You are not far from the Kingdom of God."

And no one dared to ask him any more questions.

MARK 12: 28-34

ST. FRANCIS DE SALES

"Just as God created 'man in his own image and likeness' so also has he ordained for man a love in the image and likeness of the love due to his divinity" (TLG, II:170).

REFLECTION

"Why do we love ourselves in charity?," our saint asks. "Surely it is because we are God's image and likeness. Since all men have this same dignity, we also love them as ourselves, that is, in their character as the most holy and loving images of the divinity. It is in this character . . . that we are related to God by such [a] close [covenant] and such loving dependence that nothing prevents him from saying that he is our Father and from calling us his children [1Jn. 3:1–2]. It is in this character that we are capable of being united to his divine essence by enjoyment of his supreme goodness and bliss. It is in this character that we receive his grace and that our [minds] are associated with his most holy Spirit, and as it were 'are made partakers of his divine nature'" [1 Pet. 1:4]. Hence the same charity that produces acts of love of God produces at the same time those of love of neighbor. Just as Jacob saw that one and the same ladder touched heaven and earth and equally served the angels both to descend and to ascend [Gen. 28:12], so also we know that one and the same [love] reaches out to cherish both God and neighbor. Thus it raises us up to unite our spirit with God and it brings us back again to loving association with our neighbors. However, this is always on condition that we love our neighbor in as much as he is God's image and likeness, created to communicate with the divine goodness, to participate in his grace, and to enjoy his glory. . . . To love our neighbor in charity is to love God in man or man in God. It is to cherish God alone for love of himself and creatures for love of him.

"When we see our neighbor created to the image and likeness of God, should we not say to one another: 'Stop, do you see this created being, do you see how it resembles the Creator?' Should we not cast ourselves upon him, caress him and weep over him with love? . . . Why so? For love of him? . . . I say it is for love of God from whom he is, whose he is, by whom he is, in whom he is, for whom he is, whom he resembles in a most particular manner. For this reason, the love of God not only often commands love of neighbor but it produces such love and even pours it into man's heart as its resemblance and image. Just as man is God's image, so the sacred love of man for man is the true image of a heavenly love of man for God" (*TLG*, II:171).

PRAYER

Father, it is so hard at times to see your image and likeness in those we find disagreeable and unattractive. Help us to look beyond their brokenness and shortcomings and view them as you see them. In this way, we will overcome our feelings of displeasure and truly love you by loving your image in them. We ask this in Jesus' name. Amen.

GOSPEL

Jesus addressed this parable to those who were convinced of their own righteousness and despised everyone else. "Two people went up to the temple area to pray; one was a Pharisee and the other was a tax collector. The Pharisee took up his position and spoke this prayer to himself, 'O God, I thank you that I am not like the rest of humanity—greedy, dishonest, adulterous—or even like this tax collector. I fast twice a week, and I pay tithes on my whole income.' But the tax collector stood off at a distance and would not even raise his eyes to heaven but beat his breast and prayed, 'O God, be merciful to me a sinner.' I tell you, the latter went home justified, not the former; for everyone who exalts himself will be humbled, and the one who humbles himself will be exalted."

LUKE 18: 9-14

ST. FRANCIS DE SALES

"Arrogant, presumptuous minds who admire and rate themselves very high in their own esteem look down on others as base and low. 'I am not like the rest of men,' said the foolish Pharisee" (IDL, pt. 3, ch. 28).

REFLECTION

"Let us come to the penitent sinner. Without doubt we are wrong to call him a sinner, for he is no longer so, since he already detests sin. And if indeed the Holy Spirit is not yet in his heart by residence, he is there nonetheless by assistance. For who do you think gives him this repentance for having offended God if not the Holy Spirit, since we would not know how to have a good thought toward our salvation if he did not give it to us? [see 2 Cor. 3:5]. But has this poor man done anything on his part? Yes, most certainly he has. Listen to the words of David: Lord, You looked upon me when I was in the quagmire of my sin. You opened my heart and I did not close it. You have drawn me and I have not let go. You have urged me and I have not turned back [see Ps. 102:18, 20–21; 103:3–4 and Is 50:5]. We have plenty of proof that prayers of penitent sinners are agreeable to the Divine Majesty. But I shall content myself with citing the example of the publican who went up to the Temple a sinner and came down from it justified, thanks to the humble prayer he had made" (*Sermons on Prayer*, 14).

PRAYER

How moving, Lord, and refreshing is the publican's prayer that has ravished your heart! Grace me with this same attitude of humble reverence and penitence that will make me justified and pleasing in your eyes. Grant this through Jesus Christ Our Lord. Amen.

QUESTIONS FOR REFLECTION OR DISCUSSION

1. Do chance encounters do anything for you? Explain any that may have had a profound effect on you.

2. What things make you angry and why? What do you see as the basis of justified anger and zeal?

3. How would you deal with the tendency of believing that our personal problems or those of others are a sign of God's displeasure with us?

4. How do you deal with the feeling that your little, feeble efforts to do good do not really amount to much?

5. Do you harbor any ill-will toward others, especially family members? Why?

6. How do you look upon God's commandments?

7. Are there any aspects of Jesus' teaching that you tend to minimize or ignore?

8. In what way can past sins be seen as salutary and helpful?

FOURTH WEEK
OF
LENT

GOSPEL

As Jesus passed by he saw a man blind from birth. His disciples asked him, "Rabbi, who sinned, this man or his parents, that he was born blind?" Jesus answered, "Neither he nor his parents sinned; it is so that the works of God might be made visible through him. We have to do the works of the one who sent me while it is day. Night is coming when no one can work. While I am in the world, I am the light of the world." When he had said this, he spat on the ground and made clay with the saliva, and smeared the clay on his eyes, and said to him, "Go wash in the Pool of Siloam" —which means Sent. So he went and washed, and came back able to see.

His neighbors and those who had seen him earlier as a beggar said, "Isn't this the one who used to sit and beg?" Some said, "It is," but others said, "No, he just looks like him." He said, "I am." So they said to him, "How were your eyes opened?" He replied, "The man called Jesus made clay and anointed my eyes and told me, 'Go to Siloam and wash.' So I went there and washed and was able to see." And they said to him, "Where is he?" He said, "I don't know."

They brought the one who was once blind to the Pharisees. Now Jesus had made clay and opened his eyes on a sabbath. So then the Pharisees also asked him how he was able to see. He said to them, "He put clay on my eyes, and I washed, and now I can see." So some of the Pharisees said, "This man is not from God, because he does not keep the sabbath." But others said, "How can a sinful man do such signs?" And there was a division among them. So they said to the blind man again, "What do you have to say about him, since he opened your eyes?" He said, "He is a prophet."

Now the Jews did not believe that he had been blind and gained his sight until they summoned the parents of the one who had gained his sight. They asked them, "Is this your son, who you say was born blind? How does he now see?" His parents answered and said, "We know that this is our son and that he was born blind. We do not know how he sees now, nor do we know who opened his eyes. Ask him, he is of age; he can speak for himself." His parents said this because they were afraid of the Jews, for the Jews had already agreed that if anyone acknowledged him as the Christ, he would be expelled from the synagogue. For this reason his parents said, "He is of age; question him."

So a second time they called the man who had been blind and said to him, "Give God the praise! We know that this man is a sinner." He replied, "If he is a sinner, I do not know. One thing I do know is that I was blind and now I see." So they said to him, "What did he do to you? How did he open your eyes?" He answered them, "I told you already and you did not listen. Why do you want to hear it again? Do you want to become his disciples, too?" They ridiculed him and said, "You are that man's disciple; we are disciples of Moses! We know that God spoke to Moses, but we do not know where this one is from." The man answered and said to them, "This is what is so amazing, that you do not know where he is from, yet he opened my eyes. We know that God does not listen to sinners, but if one is devout and does his will, he listens to him. It is unheard of that anyone ever opened the eyes of a person born blind. If this man were not from God, he would not be able to do anything." They answered and said to him, "You were born totally in sin, and are you trying to teach us?" Then they threw him out.

When Jesus heard that they had thrown him out, he found him and said, "Do you believe in the Son of Man?" He answered and said, "Who is he, sir, that I may believe in him?" Jesus said to him, "You have seen him, the one speaking with you is he." He said, "I do believe, Lord," and he worshiped him. Then Jesus said, "I came into this world for judgment, so that those who do not see might see, and those who do see might become blind."

Some of the Pharisees who were with him heard this and said to him, "Surely we are not also blind, are we?" Jesus said to them, "If you were blind, you would have no sin; but now you are saying, 'We see,' so your sin remains."

JOHN 9: 1-41

Shorter form: JOHN 9:1, 6-9, 13-17, 34-38
Longer form may be optionally read on any day in the fourth week of Lent

ST. FRANCIS DE SALES

"[Physical defects] make us more highly esteem complete and perfect works, provoke us to philosophize and to have many good thoughts. In a word, they have a place in the world like shadows in a picture which give grace to it and seem to lighten up the painting" (TLG, I:110).

REFLECTION

Some art instructors have their students begin by drawing not the objects themselves but their shadows. In this way, by concentrating on the shadows, it can help us overcome our blind spots and better appreciate the light. Today's Gospel story of Jesus curing the man blind from birth draws our attention to shadows, to the shadows of physical evil, like blindness, and moral evil to make us more sensitive to the light of Christ, who calls himself "the Light of the world." Our saint expresses this idea in this way: "In a word, they have a place in the world like shadows in a picture to grace it and seem to lighten up the painting." Try as we might, it is very difficult for us to see any sense in all the evil that surrounds us, especially the horrible maiming and killing of innocent people and children by suicide bombers. Our sense of bewilderment and bafflement in the face of the mystery of evil is reflected in the question the disciples put to Jesus, "Rabbi, was it his sin or his parents that caused him to be born blind?" Jesus answers that this evil is not the result of anyone's personal sin, either this man's or his parents. People of his day, and many in our own, view physical evil and suffering as a punishment for sin. But Jesus tells them that this is not necessarily so, and his answer—to make manifest the goodness of God—does not make it any easier to see any sense in the evil that surrounds us.

There are those who out of force of habit or natural inclination only see the shadows, the evil in the world, without coming to see and understand the light much better. There are those that never see the shadows; they are blind to the evil that is in the world—the evil of starvation, the ravages of war, of child abuse, of elective abortion, and all kinds of injustices visited upon the innocent, the weak and the unsuspecting.

We see in this dramatic story of how a man who sat in darkness, in the shadows, was brought to see the light, not only the physical light but the spiritual light. Ironically, it is also a tale of those who thought they saw (the Pharisees) but were blinding themselves to the light and plunging themselves and others into darkness. The story begins with a blind man who gained his sight; it ends with the Pharisees who become spiritually blind. It tells us that contact with Christ can either cure our blindness and help us see as God sees or make us even more blind. Christ the light can either make us see or blind us. The choice is ours.

PRAYER

Father, let us not be mesmerized by the shadows of evil. May they make us more sensitive and aware of your light of truth and justice so that we might shed this light upon the shadows of evil by taking whatever actions we can to overcome them and become what you have called us to be—"the light of the world." We ask this through Christ Our Lord. Amen.

GOSPEL

JESUS SAID TO NICODEMUS:

"Just as Moses lifted up the serpent in the desert, so must the Son of Man be lifted up, so that everyone who believes in him may have eternal life."

For God so loved the world that he gave his only Son, so that everyone who believes in him might not perish but might have eternal life.   For God did not send his Son into the world to condemn the world, but that the world might be saved through him. Whoever believes in him will not be condemned, but whoever does not believe has already been condemned, because he has not believed in the name of the only Son of God. And this is the verdict, that the light came into the world, but people preferred darkness to light, because their works were evil. For everyone who does wicked things hates the light and does not come toward the light, so that his works might not be exposed. But whoever lives the truth comes to the light, so that his works may be clearly seen as done in God.

JOHN 3: 14-21

ST. FRANCIS DE SALES

"All [except the Virgin Mary] have been bitten by this serpent. Now this bite was so venomous that we would all have died an eternal death if God had not provided against such a misfortune. . . . Therefore, he ordained that his Son should die and be that serpent placed on the pole of the cross to be gazed upon by all that had been bitten and sullied by sin" (Lenten Sermons, 179–80).

REFLECTION

Seeking to appreciate the depth of meaning of one of the most frequently cited Gospel verses, Jn. 3:16, "God so loved the world," our saint makes this reflection: "Our Lord chose death on the cross [Ph. 2:8] to demonstrate his love for us, all the more so that the love which he had for us could not be sufficient by choosing a less rigorous death. The more one loves, the more one desires to suffer for the beloved. Oh! We must not think that Our Lord wanted to die only to redeem us, for one of his sighs alone, because of the dignity and worth of the One sighing, would suffice to save us and deliver us form 'the hands of our enemies' [Lk. 1:74]. But this infinite love could not be content unless he died out love itself. Nothing so gives witness to love as to give one's life for the beloved, as Our Lord himself said [Jn. 15:3]. How remarkable it is that God loved us so much to allow his son to die for us, who deserved death. [Jn. 3:16; Rm. 5:8]. Our Lord was not content to die a common death for us but chose the greatest abjection and ignominy which one could ever imagine. Oh! God, how admirable are your secret judgments and how incomprehensible [Rm. 11:33]. The ones we know are very great and admirable, but all the more so are those beyond compare that we do not know. The Son of God is nailed to a cross. And who put him there? Without a doubt, it was love. Now, since it is certain that he died out of love for us, the least we can do for him is to live by loving [2 Cor. 5:14]. Nothing is impossible for love [see St. Augustine, Sermon 7, 3; S. Bernard, Sermon 1,4 for Palm Sunday]; it will destroy all that is in us that is displeasing to the Divine Majesty" (*OEA*, 9:39–40).

PRAYER

Father, we can never fully appreciate the length and depth of your love for us. But it is by lovingly taking up our daily crosses—those little inconvenient sufferings, frustrations and disappointments —that we can show our love for you and come closer to understanding how much you love us. Amen.

GOSPEL

Tax collectors and sinners were all drawing near to listen to Jesus, but the Pharisees and scribes began to complain, saying, "This man welcomes sinners and eats with them."

So to them Jesus addressed this parable: "A man had two sons, and the younger son said to his father, 'Father, give me the share of your estate that should come to me.' So the father divided the property between them. After a few days, the younger son collected all his belongings and set off to a distant country where he squandered his inheritance on a life of dissipation. When he had freely spent everything, a severe famine struck that country, and he found himself in dire need. So he hired himself out to one of the local citizens who sent him to his farm to tend the swine. And he longed to eat his fill of the pods on which the swine fed, but nobody gave him any. Coming to his senses he thought, 'How many of my father's hired workers have more than enough food to eat, but here am I, dying from hunger. I shall get up and go to my father and I shall say to him, "Father, I have sinned against heaven and against you. I no longer deserve to be called your son; treat me as you would treat one of your hired workers."' So he got up and went back to his father. While he was still a long way off, his father caught sight of him, and was filled with compassion. He ran to his son, embraced him and kissed him. His son said to him, 'Father, I have sinned against heaven and against you; I no longer deserve to be called your son.' But his father ordered his servants, 'Quickly, bring the finest robe and put it on him; put a ring on his finger and sandals on his feet. Take the fattened calf and slaughter it. Then let us celebrate with a feast, because this son of mine was dead, and has come to life again; he was lost, and has been found.' Then the celebration began. Now the older son had been out in the field and, on his way back, as he neared the house, he heard the sound of music and dancing. He called one of the servants and asked what this might mean. The servant said to him, 'Your brother has returned and your father has slaughtered the fattened calf because he has him back safe and sound.' He became angry, and when he refused to enter the house, his father came out and pleaded with him. He said to his father in reply, 'Look, all these years I served you and not once did I disobey your orders; yet you never gave me even a young goat to feast on with my friends. But when your son returns who swallowed up your property with prostitutes, for him you slaughter the fattened calf.' He said to him, 'My son, you are here with me always; everything I have is yours. But now we must celebrate and rejoice, because your brother was dead and has come to life again; he was lost and has been found.'"

LUKE 15: 1-3, 11-32

ST. FRANCIS DE SALES

"Lord, how rich is your heart in mercy [see Ps. 86:5] and how generous in good will" (IDL, pt. 1, ch. 11).

REFLECTION

This parable known as the "Prodigal Son," but should be more aptly called "The Merciful Father," was choreographed by the greatly admired choreographer, George Balanchine, and danced by the famous Russian ballet dancer, Mikhail Baryshnikov as the Prodigal Son. Balanchine has him dance wildly as he leaves his Father to go off and live a dissolute life. And when he returns, he has the great dancer crawl on his knees to his Father, who stands, feet firmly planted apart, arms folded with a very stern and condemning look on his face. This interpretation, unfortunately, distorts the essential meaning of the parable, namely, how overjoyed and merciful the Father is in seeing his son return to him repentant. It explicitly says, "While he was still a long way off, his father caught sight of him, and was filled with compassion. He ran to his son, embraced him and kissed him." It would have been more in keeping with the parable if Balanchine had the Father dancing wildly to go out and meet his son, and once they met, to have them both dance more wildly and more jubilantly than when the son took off. That would have captured the true essence and meaning of the story.

The elder son feels that the Father is showing favoritism to his playboy brother. In reality, the Father treats each of them as individuals, according to their own personal needs. He tries to smooth things over by reminding his oldest son that the younger one is still his brother. The fact of his return should be an occasion for joy for the whole family.

In this story, Jesus invites us to resemble the Father. This parable is a moving and stirring sermon on the scriptural admonition to be merciful as the father is merciful. It means that we must be reconcilers, as God our Father is in the person of his Son. We have all been reconciled to the Father through Christ after having squandered all the spiritual gifts and blessings we have received. St. Paul reminds us that we have been given the ministry of reconciliation so that, as ambassadors of Christ, Christ appeals through us for people to be reconciled with God, the Father, and with each other.

PRAYER

"Father, because I know the mercy and love you bear me, come to meet me, open the arms of your mercy, embrace this prodigal child, give me the robe of innocence, the ring of a vibrant faith, the sandals of the example of your saints, whom I must imitate. Give me, Oh Father, the fatted calf, that is to say, your Son in the Most Holy Sacrament so that it will be nourishment for my soul." (*OEA*, 2:393). Amen.

GOSPEL

At that time Jesus left [Samaria] for Galilee. For Jesus himself testified that a prophet has no honor in his native place. When he came into Galilee, the Galileans welcomed him, since they had seen all he had done in Jerusalem at the feast; for they themselves had gone to the feast.

Then he returned to Cana in Galilee, where he had made the water wine. Now there was a royal official whose son was ill in Capernaum. When he heard that Jesus had arrived in Galilee from Judea, he went to him and asked him to come down and heal his son, who was near death. Jesus said to him, "Unless you people see signs and wonders, you will not believe." The royal official said to him, "Sir, come down before my child dies." Jesus said to him, "You may go; your son will live." The man believed what Jesus said to him and left. While the man was on his way back, his slaves met him and told him that his boy would live. He asked them when he began to recover. They told him, "The fever left him yesterday, about one in the afternoon." The father realized that just at that time Jesus had said to him, "Your son will live," and he and his whole household came to believe. Now this was the second sign Jesus did when he came to Galilee from Judea.

JOHN 4: 43-54

ST. FRANCIS DE SALES

"If some mishap strikes terror into our heart, it immediately turns to the divinity. It thus attests that when everything goes ill with it, he alone is good to it, and that when it is in danger, he alone, as its sovereign good, can save and protect it" (TLG, I:90–91).

137

REFLECTION

Our sense of need is an indication that we are basically oriented toward God in our very nature. It makes us realize that we are fundamentally relational creatures, insufficient in ourselves to achieve the end for which we were created. The deeper the need, the more acute is our felt insufficiency and incompleteness. For our saint, this experience points to our being 'wired' for God. He expresses it in this way: "If some mishap strikes terror into our heart, it immediately turns to the divinity. It thus attests that when everything goes ill with it, he alone is good to it, and that when it is in danger, he alone, as its sovereign good, can save and protect it." This describes perhaps the inner turmoil the royal official experienced as he saw himself helpless, despite whatever material resources or political clout he might have had, in the face of the imminent death of his son. Deep down in his heart, he knew that there was no earthly power that could heal and save his son from death. Upon hearing about the extraordinary miracles that this humble carpenter from Nazareth performed, he swallowed his pride and felt the need to beg for his son's life from one whom he suspected was especially gifted by a transcendent power, by God. No doubt, the royal official had to withstand the ridicule and the taunts of his peers for lowering himself by approaching an itinerant preacher. But he did not let these stand in the way and was richly rewarded for his courage, humility, and faith. He personally and gratefully experienced the power of God's healing word that not only healed his son but brought him and his whole household to faith in Jesus.

PRAYER

Merciful Father, my faith and courage in you are weak and halting. Encouraged by the many gifts and blessings you have given and continue to give me, may my faith in your merciful kindness grow stronger and stronger. I make this prayer through Jesus Christ, your Son. Amen.

GOSPEL

There was a feast of the Jews, and Jesus went up to Jerusalem. Now there is in Jerusalem at the Sheep Gate a pool called in Hebrew Bethesda, with five porticoes. In these lay a large number of ill, blind, lame, and crippled. One man was there who had been ill for thirty-eight years. When Jesus saw him lying there and knew that he had been ill for a long time, he said to him, "Do you want to be well?" The sick man answered him, "Sir, I have no one to put me into the pool when the water is stirred up; while I am on my way, someone else gets down there before me." Jesus said to him, "Rise, take up your mat, and walk." Immediately the man became well, took up his mat, and walked.

Now that day was a sabbath. So the Jews said to the man who was cured, "It is the sabbath, and it is not lawful for you to carry your mat." He answered them, "The man who made me well told me, 'Take up your mat and walk.'" They asked him, "Who is the man who told you, 'Take it up and walk'?" The man who was healed did not know who it was, for Jesus had slipped away, since there was a crowd there. After this Jesus found him in the temple area and said to him, "Look, you are well; do not sin any more, so that nothing worse may happen to you." The man went and told the Jews that Jesus was the one who had made him well. Therefore, the Jews began to persecute Jesus because he did this on a sabbath.

JOHN 5: 1-16

ST. FRANCIS DE SALES

"[God] has planted in men's hearts a special natural inclination not only to love God in general, but to love in particular and above all things his divine goodness, which is better and more lovable than all things" (TLG, I:93).

REFLECTION

Our saint was firmly convinced that we have a natural inclination to love God above all things. However, our nature has been deeply wounded by original sin and cannot follow this inclination on its own. He believed that sin has weakened our will more than it has darkened our intellect. He illustrates how sin thwarts our efforts to actualize this inclination. "Eagles have strong hearts and great power of flight, yet they have immeasurably more sight than flight, and they extend their vision much more quickly and much farther than their wings. So too minds; since they are animated by a holy natural inclination towards God, they have far more light in the intellect for seeing how worthy of love the godhead is than strength of will for loving it. Sin has weakened the human will far more than it has darkened the intellect. That rebellion of the [sense] appetite that we call concupiscence does indeed disturb the intellect, but it is against the will that it chiefly stirs up sedition and revolt. Hence the poor will, already very weak, is shaken by the continual assaults that concupiscence launches against it and it cannot make as much progress in divine love as reason and natural inclination indicate I should . . .

"Our wretched nature, corrupted as it is by sin, is like the palm trees we have here [in Annecy]. They put forth certain imperfect products, attempts at fruit as it were, but it is reserved for trees in warmer countries to bear whole, ripe, seasoned dates. So too this human heart of ours in the most natural way produces certain beginnings of love for God. But to advance as far as loving him above all things, which is the true maturity of love owed to such supreme goodness, belongs only to hearts animated and assisted by heavenly grace and in the state of holy charity. This slight imperfect love, whose stirrings are felt by nature, is only a sort of will without will, a will which would will but does not will, a sterile will, which produces no true effects, a paralytic will that sees the healthful pool of holy love but does not have the strength to throw itself into the life of generous vigor needed effectively to prefer God above all other things. Speaking in the person of the sinner, the apostle cries out [Rm. 7:18] concerning such a will: 'To wish is within my power, but I do not find the strength to accomplish what is good'" (*TLG*, I:97).

PRAYER

Lord, we are paralyzed by our sins and unable on our own to plunge into the healing pool of your merciful love. To find the power to do this, we must be willing like the paralytic to want to be healed of our sinfulness and call incessantly upon your help. Grant this through Christ Our Lord. Amen.

GOSPEL

Jesus answered the Jews: "My Father is at work until now, so I am at work." For this reason they tried all the more to kill him, because he not only broke the sabbath but he also called God his own father, making himself equal to God.

Jesus answered and said to them, "Amen, amen, I say to you, the Son cannot do anything on his own, but only what he sees the Father doing; for what he does, the Son will do also. For the Father loves the Son and shows him everything that he himself does, and he will show him greater works than these, so that you may be amazed. For just as the Father raises the dead and gives life, so also does the Son give life to whomever he wishes. Nor does the Father judge anyone, but he has given all judgment to the Son, so that all may honor the Son just as they honor the Father. Whoever does not honor the Son does not honor the Father who sent him. Amen, amen, I say to you, whoever hears my word and believes in the one who sent me has eternal life and will not come to condemnation, but has passed from death to life. Amen, amen, I say to you, the hour is coming and is now here when the dead will hear the voice of the Son of God, and those who hear will live. For just as the Father has life in himself, so also he gave to the Son the possession of life in himself. And he gave him power to exercise judgment, because he is the Son of Man. Do not be amazed at this, because the hour is coming in which all who are in the tombs will hear his voice and will come out, those who have done good deeds to the resurrection of life, but those who have done wicked deeds to the resurrection of condemnation.

"I cannot do anything on my own; I judge as I hear, and my judgment is just, because I do not seek my own will but the will of the one who sent me."

JOHN 5: 17-30

ST. FRANCIS DE SALES

"When we spend ourselves, what we do by our own choice or our own will always greatly satisfies our self-love. But to allow ourselves to be spent for the neighbor in things which she wishes and we do not, that is, which we do not choose, therein lies the sovereign degree of abnegation which Our Lord and Master taught us in dying . . . It is always of greater value by far to do what we are made to do (I mean, of course, only in that which is not contrary to God and does not offend Him) than to do what we choose of ourselves" (Lenten Sermons, 94–95).

REFLECTION

St. Francis de Sales stresses the necessity of dying to our own will. "One day the great St. Basil, while considering this truth, asked himself: 'Would it not be possible to serve God perfectly by performing great and harsh penances and austerities, indeed great works for Our Lord, while doing our own will?' [*Regulae Breviores*, 115–20]. And immediately afterwards, he imagined that Our Lord and most holy Master answered: 'I emptied myself of my own glory; I came down from heaven; I took upon myself all human miseries, and finally I died, by a death on a cross [Ph. 2:7]. And why did I do that? Perhaps to suffer and by this means to save mankind or, perhaps, I did it by my own choice? Oh no!, pardon me, the only reason why I did all that I did was to submit my will to my Father, who desired it. And to show that it was not by my choice, you should know that if my Father's will had been that I die in another way than that of the cross or else that I would live any easy life, I would have found myself as prompt as I was because I have not come into the world to do my will, but that of my Father who sent me' [Jn. 5:30; 6:38; Ps. 34:9; Rm. 15:3]. Oh God, if our dear Savior, whose will could never be anything but always most perfect, and also could not chose anything which was not very pleasing to his Father, did not want to live in any other way, why do we then have the audacity to have our will live, whose choices ordinarily spoil all our works" (*OEA*, 9:86–87).

PRAYER

Lord, we stubbornly cling to our own will and freedom falsely believing in our complete autonomy. Teach us through the example of our crucified and risen Lord that true freedom and peace are found in our loving obedience to your will. We ask this in Jesus' name. Amen.

GOSPEL

JESUS SAID TO THE JEWS:

"If I testify on my own behalf, my testimony is not true. But there is another who testifies on my behalf, and I know that the testimony he gives on my behalf is true. You sent emissaries to John, and he testified to the truth. I do not accept human testimony, but I say this so that you may be saved. He was a burning and shining lamp, and for a while you were content to rejoice in his light. But I have testimony greater than John's. The works that the Father gave me to accomplish, these works that I perform testify on my behalf that the Father has sent me. Moreover, the Father who sent me has testified on my behalf. But you have never heard his voice nor seen his form, and you do not have his word remaining in you, because you do not believe in the one whom he has sent. You search the Scriptures, because you think you have eternal life through them; even they testify on my behalf. But you do not want to come to me to have life.

"I do not accept human praise; moreover, I know that you do not have the love of God in you. I came in the name of my Father, but you do not accept me; yet if another comes in his own name, you will accept him. How can you believe, when you accept praise from one another and do not seek the praise that comes from the only God? Do not think that I will accuse you before the Father: the one who will accuse you is Moses, in whom you have placed your hope. For if you had believed Moses, you would have believed me, because he wrote about me. But if you do not believe his writings, how will you believe my words?"

JOHN 5: 31-47

ST. FRANCIS DE SALES

"A great part of the evil that exists among Christians today comes from the fact that they believe those whom they should not believe, and they do not believe in those they should believe" (OEA, 7:120).

REFLECTION

"Our Lord, after having predicted it on many occasions, still wants to demonstrate his mission and always boasts of it, saying: 'As the Father sent me' [Jn. 20:21; 6:58]; 'My teaching is not mine but his who sent me [Jn. 7:16]. 'You know me and you know where I come from and I do not come of myself.' See how he boasts of his mission, of which he had no need of giving any other proof but Scripture, for he had been so explicitly predicted that one could easily recognize it. All the prophets speak only of him in such a way that he could unequivocally say: 'Search the Scriptures; they give testimony to me' [Jn. 5:39]. Despite all of this, he was not content to say that he had been sent nor to prove his mission by Scripture alone; he wanted clear and perceptible testimony of his Father—at his baptism [Mt. 3:17] and at his Transfiguration [Mt. 17:5; Lk. 9:35]: 'This is my beloved Son in whom I am well-pleased. Listen to him.' And again in Jn. 12:28: 'I have glorified [your name] and will again glorify it again.' He attests to his mission by miracles and protests that without the miracles his mission was not adequately proven to the people in such a way that he says in Jn. 14:10: 'The words I speak I do not speak on my own.' And shortly afterwards: 'Believe because of the works that I do." And in Jn. 15;24: 'If I have not done among you the works that no one else has done, they would not have sin'" (*OEA*, 7:123–24).

PRAYER

We know and believe, Lord, you have been sent by the Father to love and save us from ourselves and our sinfulness. May your precious words penetrate deeply into the ears of our hearts so that we may do whatever is pleasing to you. We ask this in Jesus' name. Amen.

GOSPEL

Jesus moved about within Galilee; he did not wish to travel in Judea, because the Jews were trying to kill him. But the Jewish feast of Tabernacles was near.

But when his brothers had gone up to the feast, he himself also went up, not openly but as it were in secret.

Some of the inhabitants of Jerusalem said, "Is he not the one they are trying to kill? And look, he is speaking openly and they say nothing to him. Could the authorities have realized that he is the Christ? But we know where he is from. When the Christ comes, no one will know where he is from." So Jesus cried out in the temple area as he was teaching and said, "You know me and also know where I am from. Yet I did not come on my own, but the one who sent me, whom you do not know, is true. I know him, because I am from him, and he sent me." So they tried to arrest him, but no one laid a hand upon him, because his hour had not yet come.

JOHN 7: 1-2, 10, 25-30

ST. FRANCIS DE SALES

"Whoever alleges an extraordinary mission must prove it for what criterion shall one use if one simply claims to have it. And so Moses, St. John the Baptist and even Our Lord demonstrate it" (OEA, 7:125).

REFLECTION

Stereotyping or categorizing or putting people in pigeon holes comes to us naturally because this is the way our mind normally works. It can be helpful to understand things and persons in a general way, but it is also fraught with danger because there is an individual quality in each human person that is not readily accessible or understandable from external appearances. We think we know a person when we know something about his background—his parents, the kind of work he does, where he lives, etc. At most, this gives us a mere superficial understanding of a person. This is the kind of understanding that the people of Jerusalem and others who saw Jesus perform miracles and teach had of him. They were puzzled and suspected that he might be the Messiah, especially when the religious leaders, "the authorities," allowed him to continue to preach openly in the Temple area. But then, they had second thoughts and recalled that Scripture says that the Messiah will have a mysterious origin and they knew, so they thought, Jesus' origin. So this fact made them readily conclude that he couldn't be the Messiah. But this is precisely what they did not know and which Jesus wanted to impress on them. Yes, on one level he came from Nazareth and was a carpenter, but Jesus insists that his real origin is from the Father, who sent him and has attested by numerous signs and wonders that Jesus is from God and is God. So to truly understand who Jesus is, we need during the Lenten season to ponder with deep faith and reflect on his words and on his working in our lives and in our world.

PRAYER

Lord, open my mind and soften my heart so that I may have a deeper knowledge and appreciation of who you are and why you are who you are. Grant this through Christ Our Lord. Amen.

GOSPEL

Some in the crowd who heard these words of Jesus said, "This is truly the Prophet." Others said, "This is the Christ." But others said, "The Christ will not come from Galilee, will he? Does not Scripture say that the Christ will be of David's family and come from Bethlehem, the village where David lived?" So a division occurred in the crowd because of him. Some of them even wanted to arrest him, but no one laid hands on him.

So the guards went to the chief priests and Pharisees, who asked them, "Why did you not bring him?" The guards answered, "Never before has anyone spoken like this man." So the Pharisees answered them, "Have you also been deceived? Have any of the authorities or the Pharisees believed in him? But this crowd, which does not know the law, is accursed." Nicodemus, one of their members who had come to him earlier, said to them, "Does our law condemn a man before it first hears him and finds out what he is doing?" They answered and said to him, "You are not from Galilee also, are you? Look and see that no prophet arises from Galilee."

Then each went to his own house.

JOHN 7: 40-53

ST. FRANCIS DE SALES

"Our confession of faith is not so much an act of intellect and of faith as an act of the will and love of God" (TLG, II:40).

REFLECTION

A good deal of John's Gospel is focused on the notion of how people come to believe—how they get faith—or in the case of the passages read yesterday and today, why some just don't "get it" when it comes to faith in Jesus. For those who were properly disposed, Jesus was a "prophet" or the "Christ," the long-awaited Messiah. To them Jesus is saying by believing in me, you will be able to do the works that I do and even greater works (see Jn. 14:12). These works, of course, were those of satisfying the thirst for goodness, integrity and holiness in people. Imagine how these words rang in the ears of those who believed in him. It's not the kind of talk or encouragement that the people heard from their religious leaders. No wonder the temple guards, who were explicitly sent by the Sanhedrin to arrest Jesus and bring him in, failed to do so because they were spell bound by his words. They said to the chief priests and Pharisees: "Never before has anyone spoken like this man." Of course, these words fell on the deaf ears of the religious leaders who didn't "get it" and were contemptuous of the guards and dressed them down for being deceived and taken in by Jesus, whom they considered to be an impostor. Nicodemus appears to be the exception. He publicly and courageously defends Jesus against those who claimed to know the law but manipulated it for their own evil purposes. This incident is a constant reminder of how we conceive of Jesus, of examining our faith in him to see if it really is aligned to the way he saw himself, his relationship to the Father and to us.

PRAYER

You have given us, Lord, the gift of faith. As we ponder your words, may our faith deepen and grow so that it may be vibrant, courageous and be expressed in works of love. We ask this in Jesus' name. Amen.

QUESTIONS FOR REFLECTION
OR DISCUSSION

1. What image of God the Father does Jesus reveal in the parable of Prodigal Son?

2. Do you agree or disagree with St. Francis de Sales that we have a natural inclination to love God above all things? Explain.

3. Why do you think it was so difficult for the religious leaders to believe and accept Jesus as the Messiah? Would you have had the same difficulty?

4. In what areas do you find it difficult to accept and follow God's known will? Why?

5. How does Jesus' teaching help us to avoid negatively stereotyping people?

6. What connections do you see between love and belief?

GOSPEL

Now a man was ill, Lazarus from Bethany, the village of Mary and her sister Martha. Mary was the one who had anointed the Lord with perfumed oil and dried his feet with her hair; it was her brother Lazarus who was ill. So the sisters sent word to Jesus saying, "Master, the one you love is ill." When Jesus heard this he said, "This illness is not to end in death, but is for the glory of God, that the Son of God may be glorified through it." Now Jesus loved Martha and her sister and Lazarus. So when he heard that he was ill, he remained for two days in the place where he was. Then after this he said to his disciples, "Let us go back to Judea." The disciples said to him, "Rabbi, the Jews were just trying to stone you, and you want to go back there?" Jesus answered, "Are there not twelve hours in a day? If one walks during the day, he does not stumble, because he sees the light of this world. But if one walks at night, he stumbles, because the light is not in him." He said this, and then told them, "Our friend Lazarus is asleep, but I am going to awaken him." So the disciples said to him, "Master, if he is asleep, he will be saved." But Jesus was talking about his death, while they thought that he meant ordinary sleep. So then Jesus said to them clearly, "Lazarus has died. And I am glad for you that I was not there, that you may believe. Let us go to him." So Thomas, called Didymus, said to his fellow disciples, "Let us also go to die with him."

When Jesus arrived, he found that Lazarus had already been in the tomb for four days. Now Bethany was near Jerusalem, only about two miles away. And many of the Jews had come to Martha and Mary to comfort them about their brother. When Martha heard that Jesus was coming, she went to meet him; but Mary sat at home. Martha said to Jesus, "Lord, if you had been here, my brother would not have died. But even now I know that whatever you ask of God, God will give you."

Jesus said to her, "Your brother will rise." Martha said to him, "I know he will rise, in the resurrection on the last day." Jesus told her, "I am the resurrection and the life; whoever believes in me, even if he dies, will live, and everyone who lives and believes in me will never die. Do you believe this?" She said to him, "Yes, Lord. I have come to believe that you are the Christ, the Son of God, the one who is coming into the world."

When she had said this, she went and called her sister Mary secretly, saying, "The teacher is here and is asking for you." As soon as she heard this, she rose quickly and went to him. For Jesus had not yet come into the village, but was still where Martha had met him. So when the Jews who were with her in the house comforting her saw Mary get up quickly and go out, they followed her, presuming that she was going to the tomb to weep there. When Mary came to where Jesus was and saw him, she fell at his feet and said to him, "Lord, if you had been here, my brother would not have died." When Jesus saw her weeping and the Jews who had come with her weeping, he became perturbed and deeply troubled, and said, "Where have you laid him?" They said to him, "Sir, come and see." And Jesus wept. So the Jews said, "See how he loved him." But some of them said, "Could not the one who opened the eyes of the blind man have done something so that this man would not have died?"

So Jesus, perturbed again, came to the tomb. It was a cave, and a stone lay across it. Jesus said, "Take away the stone." Martha, the dead man's sister, said to him, "Lord, by now there will be a stench; he has been dead for four days." Jesus said to her, "Did I not tell you that if you believe you will see the glory of God?" So they took away the stone. And Jesus raised his eyes and said, "Father, I thank you for hearing me. I know that you always hear me; but because of the crowd here I have said this, that they may believe that you sent me." And when he had said this, he cried out in a loud voice, "Lazarus, come out!" The dead man came out, tied hand and foot with burial bands, and his face was wrapped in a cloth. So Jesus said to them, "Untie him and let him go."

Now many of the Jews who had come to Mary and seen what he had done began to believe in him.

JOHN 11: 1-45

Shorter form: JOHN 11:3-7, 17, 20-27, 33b-45
Longer form may be optionally read on any day in the fifth week of Lent

ST. FRANCIS DE SALES

"The resurrection of Lazarus was an even greater miracle [than the raising of the son of the widowed mother], it is true and was accomplished with a good deal more of ceremonies, but the Savior raised him at the request of the sisters" (OEA, *10:312).*

REFLECTION

What our saint dwells on in this Gospel narrative is the short but effective prayer that both sisters make to Jesus: "We must pray a good deal but with few words . . . These women [Martha and Mary] make known their needs in a few words . . . We should note that 'Jesus loved Martha and her sister Mary and Lazarus.' So he says: 'Our Lazarus sleeps, but I will go.'. . . But note this admirable prayer: 'The one you love is ill.' We supplicate Christ in two ways—by our misery and by our love or the mercy of God. God really needs our misery . . . and our misery needs God's mercy" (*OEA*, 8:97–99). This shows the great affinity we have for God for our mutual perfection. Not that God can in anyway be perfected. "[We] have great need and capacity to receive good," declares our saint, "and [God] has great abundance to bestow it. Nothing is so suitable to indigence as liberality and affluence, and nothing is so agreeable to generous affluence as need and indigence. The more the affluence the good possesses, the stronger is its inclination to diffuse and communicate itself. The more necessitous is poverty, the more avid it is to receive good, just as a vacuum is avid to be filled. Therefore, most sweet and admirable is the encounter of affluence and goodness. One could scarcely say which has greater contentment— abundant good in diffusing and communicating itself or defective and needful good in receiving it and drawing it to itself—had not the Lord said, 'It is more blessed to give than to receive [Acts 20:35]" (*TLG*, I:91–92). In their great need, Jesus responded compassionately to the prayers of both sisters.

PRAYER

Lord Jesus, help us to appreciate the truth as your servant Francis de Sales expresses that "the throne of [your] mercy is our misery" (*OEA*, 6:22). In our need, we cry out to you to bestow your goodness and mercy on us. May it please you to grant this. Amen.

GOSPEL

Some Greeks who had come to worship at the Passover Feast came to Philip, who was from Bethsaida in Galilee, and asked him, "Sir, we would like to see Jesus." Philip went and told Andrew; then Andrew and Philip went and told Jesus. Jesus answered them, "The hour has come for the Son of Man to be glorified. Amen, amen, I say to you, unless a grain of wheat falls to the ground and dies, it remains just a grain of wheat; but if it dies, it produces much fruit. Whoever loves his life loses it, and whoever hates his life in this world will preserve it for eternal life. Whoever serves me must follow me, and where I am, there also will my servant be. The Father will honor whoever serves me.

"I am troubled now. Yet what should I say? 'Father, save me from this hour'? But it was for this purpose that I came to this hour. Father, glorify your name." Then a voice came from heaven, "I have glorified it and will glorify it again." The crowd there heard it and said it was thunder; but others said, "An angel has spoken to him." Jesus answered and said, "This voice did not come for my sake but for yours. Now is the time of judgement on this world; now the ruler of this world will be driven out. And when I am lifted up from the earth, I will draw everyone to myself." He said this indicating the kind of death he would die.

JOHN 12: 20-33

ST. FRANCIS DE SALES

"[One] who out of self love wishes to keep his freedom in this world shall lose it in the next world, and [one] who shall lose it in this world out of love for God shall keep it for that same love in the next world" (TLG, II:278).

REFLECTION

It is a very human and understandable tendency to hold on to life and to refuse to let go. This common human struggle was experienced by Jesus himself. Although he tells us that he freely laid down his life, this was not without a tremendous struggle. He alludes to his suffering in the Garden of Gethsemane, when says, "My soul is troubled now." We see this more explicitly in Hebrews: "In the days when Christ was in the flesh, he offered prayers and supplications with loud cries and tears to God, who was able to save him from death" (5:7). Jesus poured out his heart and asked his Father to remove the chalice of suffering from him. He clearly saw the suffering that was in store for him and instinctively recoiled from it. It shows how human his life really was and how well he understands our natural reluctance to avoid death at all costs. And yet because, he did what the Father expected of him, he transformed the meaning of death not only for his followers, but for all of humanity. Jesus makes us understand that suffering and death when accepted out of love can be extremely beneficial not only for the one who suffers, but for all of humanity as well. He tells us that a grain of wheat in dying has considerable germinating or life-giving power just as his death has for all of humanity. Furthermore, he asserts that when he is lifted up on his cross of suffering, human beings will be drawn to him. History has certainly born this out because of the great love for all of humanity that this once ignominious symbol now conveys. This certainly illustrates the power of Christ's death on the cross.

During this season of Lent, we should profoundly ponder the words of Jesus: "He who loves his life loses it, while the person who hates [willing to give up], his life in this world will preserve it to life eternal." A self-centered life that is closed in on itself can be very limiting and confining and a kind of living death, whereas a life lived after the example of Jesus, namely, ("with and for others")[1]—will be rewarding not only in this life but in the unending life to come.

---

1. *God and Man*, E. Schillebeeckx, O.P., (New York: Sheed and Ward, 1969), 110.

PRAYER

Suffering and death, Father, naturally make us fearful and anxious. By gazing lovingly upon your cross, may we overcome our fear and come to understand and accept how suffering and death can be redemptive and lead to an unending life of love with you. Grant this through Christ Our Lord. Amen.

GOSPEL

Jesus went to the Mount of Olives. But early in the morning he arrived again in the temple area, and all the people started coming to him, and he sat down and taught them. Then the scribes and the Pharisees brought a woman who had been caught in adultery and made her stand in the middle. They said to him, "Teacher, this woman was caught in the very act of committing adultery. Now in the law, Moses commanded us to stone such women. So what do you say?" They said this to test him, so that they could have some charge to bring against him. Jesus bent down and began to write on the ground with his finger. But when they continued asking him, he straightened up and said to them, "Let the one among you who is without sin be the first to throw a stone at her." Again he bent down and wrote on the ground. And in response, they went away one by one, beginning with the elders. So he was left alone with the woman before him. Then Jesus straightened up and said to her, "Woman, where are they? Has no one condemned you?" She replied, "No one, sir." Then Jesus said, "Neither do I condemn you. Go, and from now on do not sin any more."

JOHN 8: 1-11

ST. FRANCIS DE SALES

"Hold your hearts full of love, but a gentle, peaceful and calm love. Look at your faults, like those of others, with compassion rather than with indignation, with more humility and than severity" (OEA, 14:79).

REFLECTION

Like some of the religious leaders of Jesus' day, we are naturally quick to judge and condemn someone whom we see committing a sinful action. In such cases where we cannot excuse the evil action, our saint advises us, "When we cannot excuse sin, let us at least make it worthy of compassion by attributing the most favorable cause we can to it, such as ignorance or weakness" (*IDL*, pt. 3, ch. 28). The religious leaders who caught the woman in an act of adultery showed little or no compassion and wanted to use her to get at Jesus and discredit him as a religious leader. It's interesting to note that the man was not brought along with the woman, thereby clearly demonstrating a double standard by placing all of the responsibility on the woman's shoulders. This rush-to-judgment posture of the religious leaders contrasts sharply with the compassionate attitude of Jesus toward the desperate woman. He knew that the woman had sinned seriously by violating the law, and along with the Scribes and Pharisees he respected the law because it was the revelation of God. But Jesus goes beyond this and makes us understand that the woman was also a part of God's revelation and that we should not be hasty in condemning and punishing her by stoning to death. He was well aware of her failures and knew that she very likely tried groping for virtue, even if she was not successful. Nonetheless, he loved her deeply and could see the possibilities that she had for virtuous living. He knew that she could become a better person and one to whom he could confidently say, "But from now on, avoid that sin."

PRAYER

Give me, Oh Lord, a compassionate, kind and understanding heart. Let me reflect on my own shortcomings and sins so that I will not be hasty in criticizing and condemning others. Grant this through Jesus Christ Our Lord and Savior. Amen.

GOSPEL

Jesus went to the Mount of Olives. But early in the morning he arrived again in the temple area, and all the people started coming to him, and he sat down and taught them. Then the scribes and the Pharisees brought a woman who had been caught in adultery and made her stand in the middle. They said to him, "Teacher, this woman was caught in the very act of committing adultery. Now in the law, Moses commanded us to stone such women. So what do you say?" They said this to test him, so that they could have some charge to bring against him. Jesus bent down and began to write on the ground with his finger. But when they continued asking him, he straightened up and said to them, "Let the one among you who is without sin be the first to throw a stone at her." Again he bent down and wrote on the ground. And in response, they went away one by one, beginning with the elders. So he was left alone with the woman before him. Then Jesus straightened up and said to her, "Woman, where are they? Has no one condemned you?" She replied, "No one, sir." Then Jesus said, "Neither do I condemn you. Go, and from now on do not sin any more."

JOHN 8: 1-11

ST. FRANCIS DE SALES

"I rejoice over the fact that you have found the occasion to practice Christian charity by forgiving the one . . . who had been disloyal to you. It is in this action that the greatest effort of courage and constancy of a noble spirit consists and draws the greatest graces from heaven" (OEA, 12:251–52).

REFLECTION

When Pope John Paul II was shot, the cover of *TIME* magazine had a picture of the Pope shaking the hand of the gunman who tried to kill him. It was a tender and moving lesson of forgiveness that made a deep impression on millions of people, Catholic and non-Catholic alike, the world over. The two of them conversed in Italian, a language that was foreign to both of them, but the reason they understood each other so well was that the real language the Pope spoke was that of love, forgiveness and reconciliation. The scene of the Pope in Rome's Ribbibia prison as well as Jesus forgiving the woman caught in adultery is a powerful reminder of Christ's fundamental teaching on forgiveness, mercy and compassion. Yet how well do we accept and practice forgiveness? Don't most of us find it extremely difficult and distasteful to forgive others, especially those very close to us—a spouse, children, brothers and sisters, neighbors, those we work with? Don't we like to harbor grudges and enjoy making people squirm and pay for the way they have treated us? We hear people say, "Yeah, there'll come a day when they will come crawling on their hands and knees to beg me for forgiveness." So we withhold our forgiveness thinking: "Nobody's going to treat me that way." "Nobody's goin' to walk all over me." "Nobody's goin' to take advantage of me," etc.

The wise man tells us that we like to "hug tightly" anger and hatred (Sir. 27:30) in the false belief, I guess, that it gives us some power over those who have wronged us or who we imagine have wronged us. But human experience teaches us otherwise. When we do not forgive, it is the other person who wields power over us and not the other way around. The *TIME* article points out in powerful language how liberating forgiveness can really be: "Forgiveness frees the forgiver. It extracts the forgiver from someone else's nightmare."[1]

---

1. Lance Morrow, TIME (Jan. 9, 1984).

It is an unforgiving and unloving heart that stunts our growth as human beings because it makes us petty, small and mean. We easily forget our origins and our roots—that we are made in God's image and likeness. The qualities of God that we can imitate are not his omniscience nor his omnipotence but, his kindness, mercy, compassion and forgiveness. To be God-like ultimately means to be more human in an ennobling sense. For we are told that the "Lord is kind and merciful, slow to anger and rich in compassion" (Ps. 103:8). Who could deny that people who are merciful, kind and forgiving are not more human in the best sense of the word?

PRAYER

Merciful Father, when we cannot excuse the sin, give us understanding hearts that move us with compassion for the sinner and to pray for the person's conversion. Grant this through Christ Our Lord. Amen.

In Year C, when the preceding Gospel is read on Sunday, the following text is used.

GOSPEL

Jesus spoke to them again, saying, "I am the light of the world. Whoever follows me will not walk in darkness, but will have the light of life." So the Pharisees said to him, "You testify on your own behalf, so your testimony cannot be verified." Jesus answered and said to them, "Even if I do testify on my own behalf, my testimony can be verified, because I know where I came from and where I am going. But you do not know where I come from or where I am going. You judge by appearances, but I do not judge anyone. And even if I should judge, my judgment is valid, because I am not alone, but it is I and the Father who sent me. Even in your law it is written that the testimony of two men can be verified. I testify on my behalf and so does the Father who sent me." So they said to him, "Where is your father?" Jesus answered, "You know neither me nor my Father. If you knew me, you would know my Father also." He spoke these words while teaching in the treasury in the temple area. But no one arrested him, because his hour had not yet come.

JOHN 8: 12-20

ST. FRANCIS DE SALES

"In the morning . . . I would consider that our amorous Savior is the 'light of the Gentiles' and the light that dissipates the darkness of sin" (OEA, 22:27).

REFLECTION

We should not be surprised at the reaction of the Scribes and Pharisees of what they believed was Jesus' preposterous claim to be the

"the Light of the World," that is, the light by which all people are to be guided by if they do not want to walk in the darkness of ignorance and sin. No other religious leader, neither Buddha, nor Confucius nor Mohammed, ever made such a startling claim. The religious leaders of Jesus' day deeply resented and rejected off hand this claim because they could see no reasonable basis for it, coming as it did from an obscure carpenter from the backwater town of Nazareth turned into a self-appointed itinerant preacher. He was not schooled in the Torah; he did not study under any rabbi. So where does he get off presenting himself as the moral and religious guide for all people to follow, and especially for those of us who have all of the credentials and teaching authority? No wonder they told him he is not giving any evidence or authority for this claim other than his own statement.

Jesus readily acknowledges that the law calls for two witnesses to be acceptable as credible. So he asserts that his Father, that is, God himself, gives witness to the truth of his statement as well as his own integrity and moral character. When asked where his Father is, Jesus simply replies by saying they do not know the Father and this is why they do not accept his teaching since they judge by appearances only. No wonder they become more befuddled, bewildered and exasperated with him. We who have the benefit of the mysterious yet far-reaching effects of the light of his teachings down through the centuries and throughout the world have come to recognize the truth and great blessings of this "Light" that shines in the darkness of monumental ignorance and enormous evil.

PRAYER

"Deliver me, Oh Father, from the darkness and the blindness of sin so that I may rejoice in the blood and the merits of your blessed Son, Jesus Christ my Lord and that I be counted among your children, who are the 'sons [and daughters] of light' [Lk. 16:8] in your kingdom" (OEA, 26:418). Amen.

GOSPEL

JESUS SAID TO THE PHARISEES:

"I am going away and you will look for me, but you will die in your sin. Where I am going you cannot come." So the Jews said, "He is not going to kill himself, is he, because he said, 'Where I am going you cannot come'?" He said to them, "You belong to what is below, I belong to what is above. You belong to this world, but I do not belong to this world. That is why I told you that you will die in your sins. For if you do not believe that I AM, you will die in your sins." So they said to him, "Who are you?" Jesus said to them, "What I told you from the beginning. I have much to say about you in condemnation. But the one who sent me is true, and what I heard from him I tell the world." They did not realize that he was speaking to them of the Father. So Jesus said to them, "When you lift up the Son of Man, then you will realize that I AM, and that I do nothing on my own, but I say only what the Father taught me. The one who sent me is with me. He has not left me alone, because I always do what is pleasing to him." Because he spoke this way, many came to believe in him.

JOHN 8: 21-30

ST. FRANCIS DE SALES

"Do we not know the word of the Lord himself: 'And I, if I be lifted up from the earth, will draw all things to myself'? Was he not lifted up on the cross? Did he not suffer?—and how then having drawn to himself the Church, should he let it escape so utterly from him? How should he let go this prize which had cost him so dear?' (The Catholic Controversy: St. Francis de Sales' Defense of the Faith, 54–55).

REFLECTION

The religious leaders keep pressing Jesus to reveal who he is and what he is about. It appears that Jesus is merely parrying their questioning thrusts to avoid giving them any definite answer. But he states quite bluntly and unequivocally "I am," thereby expressing the very name that God announced to Moses in the scene of the burning bush at the foot of Mt. Sinai. Some interpreters have seen in this response our inability to express or to capture in any name God's incomprehensibility. Yet, one insightful observation explains the statement "I am" as conveying the idea that "I am here for you." This, perhaps, can make us better understand Jesus' saying. "The 'I am he,' [Jesus] . . . expands it with a reference to the future history: 'When you have lifted up the Son of Man, then you will know that I am he (Jn 8:28).' On the cross, his Sonship, his oneness with the Father becomes visible. The cross is the true 'height.' It is the height of 'love to the end' (Jn 13:1). On the cross Jesus is exalted to the very 'height' of the God who is Love. It is there that he can be 'known', that the 'I am he' can be recognized" (Pope Benedict XVI, *Jesus of Nazareth*, 349).

So Jesus is telling the religious leaders of his day and us, we will come to know him only in connection with the cross and his crucifixion. It is on the cross that Jesus reveals his unbounded love for us, his great desire to be with us, to suffer with us and to save us.

PRAYER

"I beg you, holy Father, through your infinite mercy, through the power of that Passion which your Son so lovingly endured on the tree of the cross and through the merits and intercession of the Blessed Virgin and of all the elect since the beginning of the world, to deign to forgive our sins" (*OEA*, 26:414). Amen.

GOSPEL

Jesus said to those Jews who believed in him, "If you remain in my word, you will truly be my disciples, and you will know the truth, and the truth will set you free." They answered him, "We are descendants of Abraham and have never been enslaved to anyone. How can you say, 'You will become free'?" Jesus answered them, "Amen, amen, I say to you, everyone who commits sin is a slave of sin. A slave does not remain in a household forever, but a son always remains. So if the Son frees you, then you will truly be free. I know that you are descendants of Abraham. But you are trying to kill me, because my word has no room among you. I tell you what I have seen in the Father's presence; then do what you have heard from the Father."

They answered and said to him, "Our father is Abraham." Jesus said to them, "If you were Abraham's children, you would be doing the works of Abraham. But now you are trying to kill me, a man who has told you the truth that I heard from God; Abraham did not do this. You are doing the works of your father!" So they said to him, "We were not born of fornication. We have one Father, God." Jesus said to them, "If God were your Father, you would love me, for I came from God and am here; I did not come on my own, but he sent me."

JOHN 8: 31-42

ST. FRANCIS DE SALES

"Love has no convicts or slaves, but brings all things under its obedience by so [gentle] a force that, just as nothing is as strong as love, so nothing is worthy of love as its strength" (TLG, I: 66).

REFLECTION

Reflecting on the nature of true freedom, its relation to love, and on the slavery of sin, our saint observes: "Our free will is never so free as when it is a slave of God's will. Just as it is never so servile as when it serves its own will. It never has so much life as when it dies to itself and never so much death as when it lives to itself. We have the liberty to do good and evil, but to choose evil is not to use but to abuse this liberty. Let us renounce such wretched liberty and subject forever our free will to the rule of heavenly love. Let us become slaves to [love], whose serfs are happier than kings. If our souls should ever will to use their liberty against our resolutions to serve God eternally and without reserve, Oh, then, for love of God, let us sacrifice our free will so that it may live in God! A man who out of selfish love wishes to keep his freedom in this world shall lose it in the next world, and he who shall lose it in this world for love of God shall keep it for that same love in the next world. He who gives it liberty in this world shall find it a serf and a slave in the other world, and he who makes it serve the cross in this world shall have it free in the other world. For there when he is absorbed in God's goodness [and truth], his liberty will be converted into love and love into liberty, a liberty infinitely sweet" (*TLG*, II:277–78).

PRAYER

Lord, help us to see and appreciate the relationship between freedom and love, namely, that love can only be freely given and the only constraint or coercion that love knows is freedom. Grant this in Jesus' name. Amen.

GOSPEL

JESUS SAID TO THE JEWS:

"Amen, amen, I say to you, whoever keeps my word will never see death." So the Jews said to him, "Now we are sure that you are possessed. Abraham died, as did the prophets, yet you say, 'Whoever keeps my word will never taste death.' Are you greater than our father Abraham, who died? Or the prophets, who died? Who do you make yourself out to be?" Jesus answered, "If I glorify myself, my glory is worth nothing; but it is my Father who glorifies me, of whom you say, 'He is our God.' You do not know him, but I know him. And if I should say that I do not know him, I would be like you a liar. But I do know him and I keep his word. Abraham your father rejoiced to see my day; he saw it and was glad." So the Jews said to him, "You are not yet fifty years old and you have seen Abraham?" Jesus said to them, "Amen, amen, I say to you, before Abraham came to be, I AM." So they picked up stones to throw at him; but Jesus hid and went out of the temple area.

JOHN 8: 51-59

ST. FRANCIS DE SALES

"We will never be happy if we do not believe. It is the beginning of our happiness" (OEA, 7:74).

REFLECTION

"We will never be happy if we do not believe. It is the beginning of our happiness . . . I tell you that many prophets and kings wanted to see what you see [Lk. 10:24] for there never were prophets who did not believe. . . This blessedness is to be principally understood of faith favored by an attractive personality and confirmed by experience. Moreover, I am talking about a distinctive faith that is well explained. Nonetheless, it is not said that 'all,' but 'many,' all the more so that some prophets have had such a specific revelation of the evangelical mysteries that they seem to be more evangelists than prophets—David, Jeremiah, Isaiah, Moses. 'Abraham rejoiced to see my day; he saw and was glad.' Others have seen in a general way among whom and the apostles there is as much difference among those including the apostles who see from quite a distance and confusedly and those who see up close and distinctly. Oh what a great blessing it is to believe. 'Blessed are the eyes that see what you see,' says Our Lord. I will say all the more, 'Blessed are the eyes that see.' How many people are there that would want to see what you see? How many Catholics in Germany and England, who would want to have the conveniences of their salvation 'to see what you see' during Lent. How many people are there in India that have only had some small inkling of the Gospel by the good example of Christians doing business with them, who have converted? They have not yet had the good news that Jesus Christ was born and died for our salvation and 'rose for our glorification' [Rm. 4:25]. They have no prelate who has care of them; they have no one to lead them to believe and do good things, showing thereby their affection that they have converted by the thousands with great penitence" (*OEA*, 7:74–75).

PRAYER

Oh Father, your servant Francis de Sales helps us to focus on the great gift of faith you have so kindly and mercifully given us. Teach us how to be more open to your word from whatever source it may come. Grant this through Jesus your Son. Amen.

GOSPEL

The Jews picked up rocks to stone Jesus. Jesus answered them, "I have shown you many good works from my Father. For which of these are you trying to stone me?" The Jews answered him, "We are not stoning you for a good work but for blasphemy. You, a man, are making yourself God." Jesus answered them, "Is it not written in your law, 'I said, "You are gods"'? If it calls them gods to whom the word of God came, and Scripture cannot be set aside, can you say that the one whom the Father has consecrated and sent into the world blasphemes because I said, 'I am the Son of God'? If I do not perform my Father's works, do not believe me; but if I perform them, even if you do not believe me, believe the works, so that you may realize and understand that the Father is in me and I am in the Father." Then they tried again to arrest him; but he escaped from their power.

He went back across the Jordan to the place where John first baptized, and there he remained. Many came to him and said, "John performed no sign, but everything John said about this man was true." And many there began to believe in him.

JOHN 10: 31-42

ST. FRANCIS DE SALES

"When the Pharisees interrogated him, [Jesus] invoked Scripture, saying: 'This is written.' You can do the same" (OEA, 26:301).

REFLECTION

In the final days of our Lenten journey as we travel with Jesus to Jerusalem, today's Gospel can help us focus more intensely on Jesus and his claim to be divine. The importance of this claim is absolutely essential to our Christian faith. C. S. Lewis goes to the heart of the matter. He shows how illogical it is for one to say, "'I'm ready to accept Jesus as a great moral teacher, but I don't accept his claim to be God.' . . . A man who was merely a man and said the sort of things Jesus said would not be a great moral teacher. He would either be a lunatic—on a level with a man who says he is a poached egg—or else he would be the Devil of Hell. You must make your choice. Either this man was, and is, the Son of God, or else a madman or something worse . . . You can shut him up for a fool, you can spit at him and kill him as a demon; or you can fall at his feet and call him Lord and God. But let us not come up with any patronizing nonsense about his being a great human teacher. He has not left that option open to us. He did not intend to."[1]

This is very evident in his exchange with those who picked up rocks and were about to stone him to death because, as they reasoned: "You, a man, are making yourself God." So they knew exactly the claim that Jesus was making by calling himself the "Son of God" and asserting that he is one with the Father. As close as the Jews believed that God was to them, they were not ready to accept the fact that God was present in their midst in the very person, life and works of Jesus. This ran counter to everything they understood about the one true God whom they worshipped. Jesus readily understood their reluctance to accept his word. This is why he says to them, "If you do not accept my word, then look at the works that I perform in my Father's name—the curing of the crippled, the blind, raising the dead—all of these works attest to the fact "that the Father is in me and I am in the Father." Try as he might with great courage and conviction in the face of impending death, they remained unmoved by his reasoning and wanted to arrest

---

1. C. S. Lewis, *Mere Christianity,* (London: MacMillan, 1960), 40–41.

him. John contrasts the close-mindedness of the Jewish leaders, of those who presumably were well versed in God's word with those of a more simple turn of mind, the followers of John the Baptist, who understood and appreciated the works of kindness and compassion that Jesus worked and believed what the Baptist foretold about Jesus.

PRAYER

Lord, you have given us this Lenten journey to deepen our faith in you by dwelling on all the marvelous works that you are accomplishing in our lives and how you continue to work in us, through us and for us so that we may come to "Live Jesus" more intensely and more faithfully. Grant this through Jesus your Son. Amen.

GOSPEL

Many of the Jews who had come to Mary and seen what Jesus had done began to believe in him. But some of them went to the Pharisees and told them what Jesus had done. So the chief priests and the Pharisees convened the Sanhedrin and said, "What are we going to do? This man is performing many signs. If we leave him alone, all will believe in him, and the Romans will come and take away both our land and our nation." But one of them, Caiaphas, who was high priest that year, said to them, "You know nothing, nor do you consider that it is better for you that one man should die instead of the people, so that the whole nation may not perish." He did not say this on his own, but since he was high priest for that year, he prophesied that Jesus was going to die for the nation, and not only for the nation, but also to gather into one the dispersed children of God. So from that day on they planned to kill him.

So Jesus no longer walked about in public among the Jews, but he left for the region near the desert, to a town called Ephraim, and there he remained with his disciples.

Now the Passover of the Jews was near, and many went up from the country to Jerusalem before Passover to purify themselves. They looked for Jesus and said to one another as they were in the temple area, "What do you think? That he will not come to the feast?"

JOHN 11: 45-56

ST. FRANCIS DE SALES

"It was [Jesus'] vocation to be Savior. For this reason the eternal Father gave many indications of his saving mission to men, not only from patriarchs and prophets, but also from himself. Indeed, strange though it seems, he even used the mouth of the most impious and criminal . . . to make clear that saving mission" (Lenten Sermons, *184*).

REFLECTION

"Notice how eager God is to reveal the real truth of His Son's vocation. Pilate declared time and time again that Our Lord was innocent, and though he condemned him, he knew that he was not guilty of any accusation brought against him. [Mt. 27:18; Lk. 23:14; Jn. 18:38; 19:4–6]. Further, did not God announce through the high priest Caiphas—the most miserable, treacherous and disloyal man who ever lived—this great truth: that it was better to have one man die so that all might be saved? [Jn. 11:49–50]. God went out of his way to show that his Son was truly Savior and that it was necessary for him to die to save us. He even revealed this truth through the most detestable high priest who ever lived on earth. Caiphas said it, but he did not understand that he was prophesying. Yet the Lord wished to make him a prophet on that occasion, since he was then occupying the chair of the great high priest [Jn. 11:51]. Certainly most of the people knew that our Divine Master was innocent. Though they asked that he be crucified, it was because of the chief priests. For you know that when a sedition arises in a city, the mob, rightly or wrongly, takes sides of those in power. Without knowing what he was doing, Pilate had it written on the cross: Jesus the Nazarene, King of the Jews; and no matter what people said, he refused to remove it or to change its wording [Jn. 19:19; 22], for it was God's will that it should express the two causes of His Son's death. Now since God's Son was crucified for us, what remains for us at this hour but to crucify with him our flesh with its passions and desires [2 Cor. 5:14; Gal. 5:24]. For love is repaid with love alone.

This is what we had to say about the second cause: by rendering Our Lord love for love and the praises and blessings we owe Him for His Death and Passion, we will be confessing Him as our Liberator and Saviour" (*Lenten Sermons*, 185–86).

PRAYER

"Jesus, my Savior, I accept your everlasting love. I acknowledge the purchase you have made for me of a place and a habitation in this happy Jerusalem, not so much for anything else as to love and praise you forever" (*IDL*, pt. 1, ch. 17). Amen.

QUESTIONS FOR REFLECTION OR DISCUSSION

1. When do you find it most easy to pray and why?

2. What can Jesus' Agony in the Garden teach us about our passions or emotions?

3. How do you deal with the tendency to rash judge others?

4. What is the prevailing view of freedom in our society and how do you see Salesian spirituality counteracting this view?

5. What is the difference between our Christian faith and that of a Buddhist or a Hindu?

6. Why do you think the religious leaders, for the most part, were reluctant to place their faith in Jesus?

HOLY
WEEK

GOSPEL

AT THE PROCESSION WITH PALMS

When Jesus and the disciples drew near Jerusalem and came to Bethphage on the Mount of Olives, Jesus sent two disciples, saying to them, "Go into the village opposite you, and immediately you will find an ass tethered, and a colt with her. Untie them and bring them here to me. And if anyone should say anything to you, reply, 'The master has need of them.' Then he will send them at once." This happened so that what had been spoken through the prophet might be fulfilled: / *Say to daughter Zion, /"Behold, your king comes to you, / meek and riding on an ass, / and on a colt, the foal of a beast of burden."* / The disciples went and did as Jesus had ordered them. They brought the ass and the colt and laid their cloaks over them, and he sat upon them. The very large crowd spread their cloaks on the road, while others cut branches from the trees and strewed them on the road. The crowds preceding him and those following kept crying out and saying: / "Hosanna to the Son of David; / blessed is the he who comes in the name of the Lord; / hosanna in the highest." / And when he entered Jerusalem the whole city was shaken and asked, "Who is this?" And the crowds replied, "This is Jesus the prophet, from Nazareth in Galilee."

MATTHEW 21: 1-11

GOSPEL

MASS

One of the Twelve, who was called Judas Iscariot, went to the chief priests and said, "What are you willing to give me if I hand him over to you?" They paid him thirty pieces of silver, and from that time on he looked for an opportunity to hand him over.

On the first day of the Feast of Unleavened Bread, the disciples approached Jesus and said, "Where do you want us to prepare for you to eat the Passover?" He said, "Go into the city to a certain man and tell him, 'The teacher says, "My appointed time draws near; in your house I shall celebrate the Passover with my disciples."'"The disciples then did as Jesus had ordered, and prepared the Passover.

When it was evening, he reclined at table with the Twelve. And while they were eating, he said, "Amen, I say to you, one of you will betray me." Deeply distressed at this, they began to say to him one after another, "Surely it is not I, Lord?" He said in reply, "He who has dipped his hand into the dish with me is the one who will betray me. The Son of Man indeed goes, as it is written of him, but woe to that man by whom the Son of Man is betrayed. It would be better for that man if he had never been born." Then Judas, his betrayer, said in reply, "Surely it is not I, Rabbi?" He answered, "You have said so."

While they were eating, Jesus took bread, said the blessing, broke it, and giving it to his disciples said, "Take and eat; this is my body." Then he took a cup, gave thanks, and gave it to them, saying, "Drink from it, all of you, for this is my blood of the covenant, which will be shed on behalf of many for the forgiveness of sins. I tell you, from now on I shall not drink this fruit of the vine until the day when I drink it with you new in the kingdom of my Father." Then, after singing a hymn, they went out to the Mount of Olives.

Then Jesus said to them, "This night all of you will have your faith in me shaken, for it is written: / *I will strike the shepherd,* / *and the sheep of the flock will be dispersed;* / but after I have been raised up, I shall go before you to Galilee." Peter said to him in reply, "Though all may have their faith in you shaken, mine will never be." Jesus said to him, "Amen, I say to you, this very night before the cock crows, you will deny me three times." Peter said to him, "Even though I should have to die with you, I will not deny you." And all the disciples spoke likewise.

Then Jesus came with them to a place called Gethsemane, and he said to his disciples, "Sit here while I go over there and pray." He took along Peter and the two sons of Zebedee, and began to feel sorrow and distress. Then he said to them, "My soul is sorrowful even to death. Remain here and keep watch with me." He advanced a little and fell prostrate in prayer, saying, "My Father, if it is possible, let this cup pass from me; yet, not as I will, but as you will." When he returned to his disciples he found them asleep. He said to Peter, "So you could not keep watch with me for one hour? Watch and pray that you may not undergo the test. The spirit is willing, but the flesh is weak." Withdrawing a second time, he prayed again, "My Father, if it is not possible that this cup pass without my drinking it, your will be done!" Then he returned once more and found them asleep, for they could not keep their eyes open. He left them and withdrew again and prayed a third time, saying the same thing again. Then he returned to his disciples and said to them, "Are you still sleeping and taking your rest? Behold, the hour is at hand when the Son of Man is to be handed over to sinners. Get up, let us go. Look, my betrayer is at hand."

While he was still speaking, Judas, one of the Twelve, arrived, accompanied by a large crowd, with swords and clubs, who had come from the chief priests and the elders of the people. His betrayer had arranged a sign with them, saying, "The man I shall kiss is the one; arrest him." Immediately he went over to Jesus and said, "Hail, Rabbi!" and he kissed him. Jesus answered him, "Friend, do what you have come for." Then stepping forward they laid hands on Jesus and arrested him. And behold, one of those who accompanied Jesus put his hand to his sword, drew it, and struck the high priest's servant, cutting off his ear. Then Jesus said to him, "Put your sword back into its sheath, for all who take the sword will perish by the sword. Do you think that I cannot call upon my Father and he will not provide me at this moment with more than twelve legions of angels? But then how would the Scriptures be fulfilled which say that it must come to pass in this way?" At that hour Jesus said to the crowds, "Have you come out as against a robber, with swords and clubs to seize me? Day after day I sat teaching in the temple area, yet you did not arrest me. But all this has come to pass that the writings of the prophets may be fulfilled." Then all the disciples left him and fled.

Those who had arrested Jesus led him away to Caiaphas the high priest, where the scribes and the elders were assembled. Peter was following him at a distance as far as the high priest's courtyard, and going inside he sat down with the servants to see the outcome. The chief priests and the entire Sanhedrin kept trying to obtain false testimony against Jesus in order to put him to death, but they found none, though many false witnesses came forward. Finally two came forward who stated, "This man said, 'I can destroy the temple of God and within three days rebuild it.'" The high priest rose and addressed him, "Have you no answer? What are these men testifying against you?" But Jesus was silent. Then the high priest said to him, "I order you to tell us under oath before the living God whether you are the Christ, the Son of God." Jesus said to him in reply, "You have said so. But I tell you: / From now on you will see 'the Son of Man / seated at the right hand of the Power' / and 'coming on the clouds of heaven.'" / Then the high priest tore his robes and said, "He has blasphemed! What further need have we of witnesses? You have now heard the blasphemy; what is your opinion?" They said in reply, "He deserves to die!" Then they spat in his face and struck him, while some slapped him, saying, "Prophesy for us, Christ: who is it that struck you?"

Now Peter was sitting outside in the courtyard. One of the maids came over to him and said, "You too were with Jesus the Galilean." But he denied it in front of everyone, saying, "I do not know what you are talking about!" As he went out to the gate, another girl saw him and said to those who were there, "This man was with Jesus the Nazorean." Again he denied it with an oath, "I do not know the man!" A little later the bystanders came over and said to Peter, "Surely you too are one of them; even your speech gives you away." At that he began to curse and to swear, "I do not know the man." And immediately a cock crowed. Then Peter remembered the word that Jesus had spoken: "Before the cock crows you will deny me three times." He went out and began to weep bitterly.

When it was morning, all the chief priests and the elders of the people took counsel against Jesus to put him to death. They bound him, led him away, and handed him over to Pilate, the governor.

Then Judas, his betrayer, seeing that Jesus had been condemned, deeply regretted what he had done. He returned the thirty pieces of silver to the chief priests and elders, saying, "I have sinned in betraying innocent blood." They said, "What is that to us? Look to it yourself." Flinging the money into the temple, he departed and went off and hanged himself. The chief priests gathered up the money, but said, "It is not lawful to deposit this in the temple treasury, for it is the price of blood." After consultation, they used it to buy the potter's field as a burial place for foreigners. That is why that field even today is called the Field of Blood. Then was fulfilled what had been said through Jeremiah the prophet, / *And they took the thirty pieces of silver, / the value of a man with a price on his head, / a price set by some of the Israelites, / and they paid it out for the potter's field / just as the Lord had commanded me.*

Now Jesus stood before the governor, who questioned him, "Are you the king of the Jews?" Jesus said, "You say so." And when he was accused by the chief priests and elders, he made no answer. Then Pilate said to him, "Do you not hear how many things they are testifying against you?" But he did not answer him one word, so that the governor was greatly amazed.

Now on the occasion of the feast the governor was accustomed to release to the crowd one prisoner whom they wished. And at that time they had a notorious prisoner called Barabbas. So when they had assembled, Pilate said to them, "Which one do you want me to release to you, Barabbas, or Jesus called Christ?" For he knew that it was out of envy that they had handed him over. While he was still seated on the bench, his wife sent him a message, "Have nothing to do with that righteous man. I suffered much in a dream today because of him." The chief priests and the elders persuaded the crowds to ask for Barabbas but to destroy Jesus. The governor said to them in reply, "Which of the two do you want me to release to you?" They answered, "Barabbas!" Pilate said to them, "Then what shall I do with Jesus called Christ?" They all said, "Let him be crucified!" But he said, "Why? What evil has he done?" They only shouted the louder, "Let him be crucified!" When Pilate saw that he was not succeeding at all, but that a riot was breaking out instead, he took water and washed his hands in the sight of the crowd, saying, "I am innocent of this man's blood. Look to it yourselves." And the whole people said in reply, "His blood be upon us and upon our children." Then he released Barabbas to them, but after he had Jesus scourged, he handed him over to be crucified.

Then the soldiers of the governor took Jesus inside the praetorium and gathered the whole cohort around him. They stripped off his clothes and threw a scarlet military cloak about him. Weaving a crown out of thorns, they placed it on his head, and a reed in his right hand. And kneeling before him, they mocked him, saying, "Hail, King of the Jews!" They spat upon him and took the reed and kept striking him on the head. And when they had mocked him, they stripped him of the cloak, dressed him in his own clothes, and led him off to crucify him.

As they were going out, they met a Cyrenian named Simon; this man they pressed into service to carry his cross.

And when they came to a place called Golgotha — which means Place of the Skull —, they gave Jesus wine to drink mixed with gall. But when he had tasted it, he refused to drink. After they had crucified him, they divided his garments by casting lots; then they sat down and kept watch over him there. And they placed over his head the written charge against him: This is Jesus, the King of the Jews. Two revolutionaries were crucified with him, one on his right and the other on his left. Those passing by reviled him, shaking their heads and saying, "You who would destroy the temple and rebuild it in three days, save yourself, if you are the Son of God, and come down from the cross!" Likewise the chief priests with the scribes and elders mocked him and said, "He saved others; he cannot save himself. So he is the king of Israel! Let him come down from the cross now, and we will believe in him. He trusted in God; let him deliver him now if he wants him. For he said, 'I am the Son of God.'" The revolutionaries who were crucified with him also kept abusing him in the same way.

From noon onward, darkness came over the whole land until three in the afternoon. And about three o'clock Jesus cried out in a loud voice, *"Eli, Eli, lema sabachthani?"* which means, "My God, my God, why have you forsaken me?" Some of the bystanders who heard it said, "This one is calling for Elijah." Immediately one of them ran to get a sponge; he soaked it in wine, and putting it on a reed, gave it to him to drink. But the rest said, "Wait, let us see if Elijah comes to save him." But Jesus cried out again in a loud voice, and gave up his spirit.

Here all kneel and pause for a short time.

And behold, the veil of the sanctuary was torn in two from top to bottom. The earth quaked, rocks were split, tombs were opened, and the bodies of many saints who had fallen asleep were raised. And coming forth from their tombs after his resurrection, they entered the holy city and appeared to many. The centurion and the men with him who were keeping watch over Jesus feared greatly when they saw the earthquake and all that was happening, and they said, "Truly, this was the Son of God!" There were many women there, looking on from a distance, who had followed Jesus from Galilee, ministering to him. Among them were Mary Magdalene and Mary the mother of James and Joseph, and the mother of the sons of Zebedee.

When it was evening, there came a rich man from Arimathea named Joseph, who was himself a disciple of Jesus. He went to Pilate and asked for the body of Jesus; then Pilate ordered it to be handed over. Taking the body, Joseph wrapped it in clean linen and laid it in his new tomb that he had hewn in the rock. Then he rolled a huge stone across the entrance to the tomb and departed. But Mary Magdalene and the other Mary remained sitting there, facing the tomb.

The next day, the one following the day of preparation, the chief priests and the Pharisees gathered before Pilate and said, "Sir, we remember that this impostor while still alive said, 'After three days I will be raised up.' Give orders, then, that the grave be secured until the third day, lest his disciples come and steal him and say to the people, 'He has been raised from the dead.' This last imposture would be worse than the first." Pilate said to them, "The guard is yours; go, secure it as best you can." So they went and secured the tomb by fixing a seal to the stone and setting the guard.

MATTHEW 26: 14-75 & 27: 1-66

Shorter form: MATTHEW 27:11-54

ST. FRANCIS DE SALES

"Not only is the ass humble, it is exceedingly patient . . . Now humility and patience have such an affinity with one another that one can hardly exist without the other . . . Finding these two qualities in this animal, Our Lord chose it rather than any other for his entry into Jerusalem" (Lenten Sermons, *171-72).*

REFLECTION

Our saint views Jesus entering Jerusalem as a triumph of his humility. This is seen by Our Lord choosing to mount an ass rather than a horse because "the ass though heavy, sluggish and lazy, has great humility. It is neither proud nor vain, in this it is unlike the haughty horse . . . Now Our Lord, who was humble and came to destroy pride, chose not to use this proud animal to carry him. He chose the most simple and the humble of all animals because He so loved holiness and humility that only a humble mount could serve him. God dwells and abides only in the simple and humble heart. [Is 57:51]. He chose the lowliness and abjection for the day of his triumph. He emptied and humbled himself. He would not have been humiliated and despised by others except he willed it. He himself emptied himself, choosing abjection. He who was the Father's equal in all things, without ceasing to remain what He was, chose to be the reproach and outcast of the people. [Ps 21 (22); Is 53:31] . . . He humbled himself, in entering Jerusalem not on a horse or other conveyance, but an ass and a colt, which were covered only with the poor mantles of his apostles. It is of this great triumph of humility that Isaiah [Is 53:3; 62:11] and Zacharias [Zach. 9:91] sing, along with that divine poet, the royal prophet David [Ps. 45:6]. He emptied himself and abased himself; He humbled himself; he came mounted on an ass and a colt. He bent his bow and darted his arrows of love into the hearts of the people of Israel. All were moved at his coming and sang: Hosanna, blessed be the Son of David, blessed is he who comes in the name of the Lord; glory be to the Most High [Ps. 117(118):26; Mt. 21:9]. His gentleness and humility captivated all their hearts. Had he come on any other conveyance he would have frightened them. This is the first quality that made the ass appropriate for Our Lord's use on this occasion: its humility" (*Lenten Sermons*, 170–71).

PRAYER

Lord, as we enter this holiest of days, help us to put on the mind and heart of Jesus, who urges us to learn from him the virtues of gentleness and humility. In contemplating his suffering and sacrifices, may we learn what true humility and gentleness are and thereby come closer to his heart. We ask this in Jesus' name. Amen.

GOSPEL

PROCESSION WITH PALMS

When Jesus and his disciples drew near to Jerusalem, to Bethpage and Bethany at the Mount of Olives, he sent two of his disciples and said to them, "Go into the village opposite you, and immediately on entering it, you will find a colt tethered on which no one has ever sat. Untie it and bring it here. If anyone should say to you, 'Why are you doing this?' reply, 'The Master has need of it and will send it back here at once.'" So they went off and found a colt tethered at a gate outside on the street, and they untied it. Some of the bystanders said to them, "What are you doing, untying the colt?" They answered them just as Jesus had told them to, and they permitted them to do it. So they brought the colt to Jesus and put their cloaks over it. And he sat on it. Many people spread their cloaks on the road, and others spread leafy branches that they had cut from the fields. Those preceding him as well as those following kept crying out: / "Hosanna! / Blessed is he who comes in the name of the Lord! / Blessed is the kingdom of our father David that is to come! / Hosanna in the highest!"

MARK 11: 1-10

Alternative: JOHN 12:12-16

GOSPEL

MASS

The Passover and the Feast of Unleavened Bread were to take place in two days' time. So the chief priests and the scribes were seeking a way to arrest him by treachery and put him to death. They said, "Not during the festival, for fear that there may be a riot among the people."

When he was in Bethany reclining at table in the house of Simon the leper, a woman came with an alabaster jar of perfumed oil, costly genuine spikenard. She broke the alabaster jar and poured it on his head. There were some who were indignant. "Why has there been this waste of perfumed oil? It could have been sold for more than three hundred days' wages and the money given to the poor." They were infuriated with her. Jesus said, "Let her alone. Why do you make trouble for her? She has done a good thing for me. The poor you will always have with you, and whenever you wish you can do good to them, but you will not always have me. She has done what she could. She has anticipated anointing my body for burial. Amen, I say to you, wherever the gospel is proclaimed to the whole world, what she has done will be told in memory of her."

Then Judas Iscariot, one of the Twelve, went off to the chief priests to hand him over to them. When they heard him they were pleased and promised to pay him money. Then he looked for an opportunity to hand him over.

On the first day of the Feast of Unleavened Bread, when they sacrificed the Passover lamb, his disciples said to him, "Where do you want us to go and prepare for you to eat the Passover?" He sent two of his disciples and said to them, "Go into a city and a man will meet you, carrying a jar of water. Follow him. Wherever he enters, say to the master of the house, 'The Teacher says, "Where is my guest room where I may eat the Passover with my disciples?"' Then he will show you a large upper room furnished and ready. Make the preparations for us there." The disciples then went off, entered the city, and found it just as he had told them; and they prepared the Passover.

When it was evening, he came with the Twelve. And as they reclined at table and were eating, Jesus said, "Amen, I say to you, one of you will betray me, one who is eating with me." They began to be distressed and to say to him, one by one, "Surely it is not I?" He said to them, "One of the Twelve, the one who dips with me into the dish. For the Son of Man indeed goes, as it is written of him, but woe to that man by whom the Son of Man is betrayed. It would be better for that man if he had never been born."

While they were eating, he took bread, said the blessing, broke it, and gave it to them, and said, "Take it; this is my body." Then he took a cup, gave thanks, and gave it to them, and they all drank from it. He said to them, "This is my blood of the covenant, which will be shed for many. Amen, I say to you, I shall not drink again the fruit of the vine until the day when I drink it new in the kingdom of God." Then, after singing a hymn, they went out to the Mount of Olives.

Then Jesus said to them, "All of you will have your faith shaken, for it is written: / *I will strike the shepherd, / and the sheep will be dispersed.* / But after I have been raised up, I shall go before you to Galilee." Peter said to him, "Even though all should have their faith shaken, mine will not be." Then Jesus said to him, "Amen, I say to you, this very night before the cock crows twice you will deny me three times." But he vehemently replied, "Even though I should have to die with you, I will not deny you." And they all spoke similarly.

Then they came to a place named Gethsemane, and he said to his disciples, "Sit here while I pray." He took with him Peter, James and John, and began to be troubled and distressed. Then he said to them, "My soul is sorrowful even to death. Remain here and keep watch." He advanced a little and fell to the ground and prayed that if it were possible the hour might pass by him; he said, "Abba, Father, all things are possible to you. Take this cup away from me, but not what I will but what you will." When he returned he found them asleep. He said to Peter, "Simon, are you asleep? Could you not keep watch for one hour? Watch and pray that you may not undergo the test. The spirit is willing but the flesh is weak." Withdrawing again, he prayed, saying the same thing. Then he returned once more and found them asleep, for they could not keep their eyes open and did not know what to answer him. He returned a third time and said to them, "Are you still sleeping and taking your rest? It is enough. The hour has come. Behold, the Son of Man is to be handed over to sinners. Get up, let us go. See, my betrayer is at hand."

Then, while he was still speaking, Judas, one of the Twelve, arrived, accompanied by a crowd with swords and clubs who had come from the chief priests, the scribes, and the elders. His betrayer had arranged a signal with them, saying, "The man I shall kiss is the one; arrest him and lead him away securely." He came and immediately went over to him and said, "Rabbi." And he kissed him. At this they laid hands on him and arrested him. One of the bystanders drew his sword, struck the high priest's servant, and cut off his ear. Jesus said to them in reply, "Have you come out as against a robber, with swords and clubs, to seize me? Day after day I was with you teaching in the temple area, yet you did not arrest me; but that the Scriptures may be fulfilled." And they all left him and fled. Now a young man followed him wearing nothing but a linen cloth about his body. They seized him, but he left the cloth behind and ran off naked.

They led Jesus away to the high priest, and all the chief priests and the elders and the scribes came together. Peter followed him at a distance into the high priest's courtyard and was seated with the guards, warming himself at the fire. The chief priests and the entire Sanhedrin kept trying to obtain testimony against Jesus in order to put him to death, but they found none. Many gave false witness against him, but their testimony did not agree. Some took the stand and testified falsely against him, alleging, "We heard him say, 'I will destroy this temple made with hands and within three days I will build another not made with hands.'" Even so their testimony did not agree. The high priest rose before the assembly and questioned Jesus, saying, "Have you no answer? What are these men testifying against you?" But he was silent and answered nothing. Again the high priest asked him and said to him, "Are you the Christ, the son of the Blessed One?" Then Jesus answered, "I am; / and *you will see the Son of Man / seated at the right hand of the Power / and coming with the clouds of heaven."* / At that the high priest tore his garments and said, "What further need have we of witnesses? You have heard the blasphemy. What do you think?" They all condemned him as deserving to die. Some began to spit on him. They blindfolded him and struck him and said to him, "Prophesy!" And the guards greeted him with blows.

While Peter was below in the courtyard, one of the high priest's maids came along. Seeing Peter warming himself, she looked intently at him and said, "You too were with the Nazarene, Jesus." But he denied it saying, "I neither know nor understand what you are talking about." So he went out into the outer court. Then the cock crowed. The maid saw him and began again to say to the bystanders, "This man is one of them." Once again he denied it. A little later the bystanders said to Peter once more, "Surely you are one of them; for you too are a Galilean." He began to curse and to swear, "I do not know this man about whom you are talking." And immediately a cock crowed a second time. Then Peter remembered the word that Jesus had said to him, "Before the cock crows twice you will deny me three times." He broke down and wept.

As soon as morning came, the chief priests with the elders and the scribes, that is, the whole Sanhedrin held a council. They bound Jesus, led him away, and handed him over to Pilate. Pilate questioned him, "Are you the king of the Jews?" He said to him in reply, "You say so." The chief priests accused him of many things. Again Pilate questioned him, "Have you no answer? See how many things they accuse you of." Jesus gave him no further answer, so that Pilate was amazed.

Now on the occasion of the feast he used to release to them one prisoner whom they requested. A man called Barabbas was then in prison along with the rebels who had committed murder in a rebellion. The crowd came forward and began to ask him to do for them as he was accustomed. Pilate answered, "Do you want me to release to you the king of the Jews?" For he knew that it was out of envy that the chief priests had handed him over. But the chief priests stirred up the crowd to have him release Barabbas for them instead. Pilate again said to them in reply, "Then what do you want me to do with the man you call the king of the Jews?" They shouted again, "Crucify him." Pilate said to them, "Why? What evil has he done?" They only shouted the louder, "Crucify him." So Pilate, wishing to satisfy the crowd, released Barabbas to them and, after he had Jesus scourged, handed him over to be crucified.

The soldiers led him away inside the palace, that is, the praetorium, and assembled the whole cohort. They clothed him in purple and, weaving a crown of thorns, placed it on him. They began to salute him with, "Hail, King of the Jews!" and kept striking his head with a reed and spitting upon him. They knelt before him in homage. And when they had mocked him, they stripped him of the purple cloak, dressed him in his own clothes, and led him out to crucify him.

They pressed into service a passer-by, Simon, a Cyrenian, who was coming in from the country, the father of Alexander and Rufus, to carry his cross. They brought him to the place of Golgotha—which is translated Place of the Skull—. They gave him wine drugged with myrrh, but he did not take it. Then they crucified him and divided his garments by casting lots for them to see what each should take. It was nine o'clock in the morning when they crucified him. The inscription of the charge against him read, "The King of the Jews." With him they crucified two revolutionaries, one on his right and one on his left. Those passing by reviled him, shaking their heads and saying, "Aha! You who would destroy the temple and rebuild it in three days, save yourself by coming down from the cross." Likewise the chief priests, with the scribes, mocked him among themselves and said, "He saved others; he cannot save himself. Let the Christ, the King of Israel, come down now from the cross that we may see and believe." Those who were crucified with him also kept abusing him. At noon darkness came over the whole land until three in the afternoon. And at three o'clock Jesus cried out in a loud voice, *"Eloi, Eloi, lema sabachthani?"* which is translated, "My God, my God, why have you forsaken me?" Some of the bystanders who heard it said, "Look, he is calling Elijah." One of them ran, soaked a sponge with wine, put it on a reed and gave it to him to drink saying, "Wait, let us see if Elijah comes to take him down." Jesus gave a loud cry and breathed his last.

Here all kneel and pause for a short time.

The veil of the sanctuary was torn in two from top to bottom. When the centurion who stood facing him saw how he breathed his last he said, "Truly this man was the Son of God!"

There were also women looking on from a distance. Among them were Mary Magdalene, Mary the mother of the younger James and of Joses, and Salome. These women had followed him when he was in Galilee and ministered to him. There were also many other women who had come up with him to Jerusalem.

When it was already evening, since it was the day of preparation, the day before the sabbath, Joseph of Arimathea, a distinguished member of the council, who was himself awaiting the kingdom of God, came and courageously went to Pilate and asked for the body of Jesus. Pilate was amazed that he was already dead. He summoned the centurion and asked him if Jesus had already died. And when he learned of it from the centurion, he gave the body to Joseph. Having bought a linen cloth, he took him down, wrapped him in the linen cloth, and laid him in a tomb that had been hewn out of the rock. Then he rolled a stone against the entrance to the tomb. Mary Magdalene and Mary the mother of Joses watched where he was laid.

MARK 14: 1-72 & 15: 1-47

Shorter form: MARK 15:1-39

ST. FRANCIS DE SALES

"Let us trust in God who is our 'Father Almighty.' By virtue of this fact all things will be rendered easy, although at first they may frighten us a little" (Lenten Sermons, 21).

REFLECTION

Those who are beginners in following Christ consider themselves to be fearless "and never feed enough on the crucifix. Nothing can satisfy them. They think of nothing but of living in tranquil rest. Nothing can overcome their courage and generosity. This is what happened to poor St. Peter. Being a mere child in the spiritual life, he made the act of generosity of getting out of the boat and walking on water and called on the Lord to save him [Mt. 14:19–31]. But he made still another later on, and it cost him dearly. For when Our Lord announced to his apostles that he was to suffer death, St. Peter, quick to speak but fainthearted and cowardly in action, boasted: 'For my part, I will never abandon you' [Mt. 26:31–35; Mk. 14:27–31; Lk. 22:33; Jn. 13:37]. And Our Lord went on, 'I shall be scourged.' 'And I too for love of thee.' 'I shall be crowned with thorns.' 'I as well.' In short he would yield in nothing to his good Master. The more Our Lord expounded on the greatness of his afflictions, the more did St. Peter passionately insist that he would do as much. But how well he realized how he had been completely deceived when he found himself, at the time of his Savior's Passion, so fainthearted and timid in the execution of his promises. It would have been much better for poor St. Peter to keep humble, relying on the power of God, than to trust vainly in the fervor which he felt at the time" (*Lenten Sermons,* 22–23).

PRAYER

In pondering your sufferings, Lord, may I come to better grasp my own weakness, inconstancy, and lack of focus. Help me to realistically appraise myself so that I trust completely in your strength. Grant this through Christ Our Lord.

GOSPEL

PROCESSION WITH PALMS

Jesus proceeded on his journey up to Jerusalem. As he drew near to Bethpage and Bethany at the place called the Mount of Olives, he sent two of his disciples. He said, "Go into the village opposite you, and as you enter it you will find a colt tethered on which no one has ever sat. Untie it and bring it here. And if anyone should ask you, 'Why are you untying it?' you will answer, 'The Master has need of it.'" So those who had been sent went off and found everything just as he had told them. And as they were untying the colt, its owners said to them, "Why are you untying this colt?" They answered, "The Master has need of it." So they brought it to Jesus, threw their cloaks over the colt, and helped Jesus to mount. As he rode along, the people were spreading their cloaks on the road; and now as he was approaching the slope of the Mount of Olives, the whole multitude of his disciples began to praise God aloud with joy for all the mighty deeds they had seen. They proclaimed: / "Blessed is the king who comes in the name of the Lord. / Peace in heaven and glory in the highest." / Some of the Pharisees in the crowd said to him, "Teacher, rebuke your disciples." He said in reply, "I tell you, if they keep silent, the stones will cry out!"

LUKE 19: 28-40

GOSPEL

MASS

When the hour came, Jesus took his place at table with the apostles. He said to them, "I have eagerly desired to eat this Passover with you before I suffer, for, I tell you, I shall not eat it again until there is fulfillment in the kingdom of God." Then he took a cup, gave thanks, and said, "Take this and share it among yourselves; for I tell you that from this time on I shall not drink of the fruit of the vine until the kingdom of God comes." Then he took the bread, said the blessing, broke it, and gave it to them, saying, "This is my body, which will be given for you; do this in memory of me." And likewise the cup after they had eaten, saying, "This cup is the new covenant in my blood, which will be shed for you.

"And yet behold, the hand of the one who is to betray me is with me on the table; for the Son of Man indeed goes as it has been determined; but woe to that man by whom he is betrayed." And they began to debate among themselves who among them would do such a deed.

Then an argument broke out among them about which of them should be regarded as the greatest. He said to them, "The kings of the Gentiles lord it over them and those in authority over them are addressed as 'Benefactors'; but among you it shall not be so. Rather, let the greatest among you be as the youngest, and the leader as the servant. For who is greater: the one seated at table or the one who serves? Is it not the one seated at table? I am among you as the one who serves. It is you who have stood by me in my trials; and I confer a kingdom on you, just as my Father has conferred one on me, that you may eat and drink at my table in my kingdom; and you will sit on thrones judging the twelve tribes of Israel.

"Simon, Simon, behold Satan has demanded to sift all of you like wheat, but I have prayed that your own faith may not fail; and once you have turned back, you must strengthen your brothers." He said to him, "Lord, I am prepared to go to prison and to die with you." But he replied, "I tell you, Peter, before the cock crows this day, you will deny three times that you know me."

He said to them, "When I sent you forth without a money bag or a sack or sandals, were you in need of anything?" "No, nothing," they replied. He said to them, "But now one who has a money bag should take it, and likewise a sack, and one who does not have a sword should sell his cloak and buy one. For I tell you that this Scripture must be fulfilled in me, namely, *He was counted among the wicked;* and indeed what is written about me is coming to fulfillment." Then they said, "Lord, look, there are two swords here." But he replied, "It is enough!"

Then going out, he went, as was his custom, to the Mount of Olives, and the disciples followed him. When he arrived at the place he said to them, "Pray that you may not undergo the test." After withdrawing about a stone's throw from them and kneeling, he prayed, saying, "Father, if you are willing, take this cup away from me; still, not my will but yours be done." And to strengthen him an angel from heaven appeared to him. He was in such agony and he prayed so fervently that his sweat became like drops of blood falling on the ground. When he rose from prayer and returned to his disciples, he found them sleeping from grief. He said to them, "Why are you sleeping? Get up and pray that you may not undergo the test."

While he was still speaking, a crowd approached and in front was one of the Twelve, a man named Judas. He went up to Jesus to kiss him. Jesus said to him, "Judas, are you betraying the Son of Man with a kiss?" His disciples realized what was about to happen, and they asked, "Lord, shall we strike with a sword?" And one of them struck the high priest's servant and cut off his right ear. But Jesus said in reply, "Stop, no more of this!" Then he touched the servant's ear and healed him. And Jesus said to the chief priests and temple guards and elders who had come for him, "Have you come out as against a robber, with swords and clubs? Day after day I was with you in the temple area, and you did not seize me; but this is your hour, the time for the power of darkness."

After arresting him they led him away and took him into the house of the high priest; Peter was following at a distance. They lit a fire in the middle of the courtyard and sat around it, and Peter sat down with them. When a maid saw him seated in the light, she looked intently at him and said, "This man too was with him." But he denied it saying, "Woman, I do not know him." A short while later someone else saw him and said, "You too are one of them"; but Peter answered, "My friend, I am not." About an hour later, still another insisted, "Assuredly, this man too was with him, for he also is a Galilean." But Peter said, "My friend, I do not know what you are talking about." Just as he was saying this, the cock crowed, and the Lord turned and looked at Peter; and Peter remembered the word of the Lord, how he had said to him, "Before the cock crows today, you will deny me three times." He went out and began to weep bitterly. The men who held Jesus in custody were ridiculing and beating him. They blindfolded him and questioned him, saying, "Prophesy! Who is it that struck you?" And they reviled him in saying many other things against him.

When day came the council of elders of the people met, both chief priests and scribes, and they brought him before their Sanhedrin. They said, "If you are the Christ, tell us," but he replied to them, "If I tell you, you will not believe, and if I question, you will not respond. But from this time on the Son of Man will be seated at the right hand of the power of God." They all asked, "Are you then the Son of God?" He replied to them, "You say that I am." Then they said, "What further need have we for testimony? We have heard it from his own mouth."

Then the whole assembly of them arose and brought him before Pilate. They brought charges against him, saying, "We found this man misleading our people; he opposes the payment of taxes to Caesar and maintains that he is the Christ, a king." Pilate asked him, "Are you the king of the Jews?" He said to him in reply, "You say so." Pilate then addressed the chief priests and the crowds, "I find this man not guilty." But they were adamant and said, "He is inciting the people with his teaching throughout all Judea, from Galilee where he began even to here."

On hearing this Pilate asked if the man was a Galilean; and upon learning that he was under Herod's jurisdiction, he sent him to Herod, who was in Jerusalem at that time. Herod was very glad to see Jesus; he had been wanting to see him for a long time, for he had heard about him and had been hoping to see him perform some sign. He questioned him at length, but he gave him no answer. The chief priests and scribes, meanwhile, stood by accusing him harshly. Herod and his soldiers treated him contemptuously and mocked him, and after clothing him in resplendent garb, he sent him back to Pilate. Herod and Pilate became friends that very day, even though they had been enemies formerly. Pilate then summoned the chief priests, the rulers, and the people and said to them, "You brought this man to me and accused him of inciting the people to revolt. I have conducted my investigation in your presence and have not found this man guilty of the charges you have brought against him, nor did Herod, for he sent him back to us. So no capital crime has been committed by him. Therefore I shall have him flogged and then release him."

But all together they shouted out, "Away with this man! Release Barabbas to us." —Now Barabbas had been imprisoned for a rebellion that had taken place in the city and for murder.— Again Pilate addressed them, still wishing to release Jesus, but they continued their shouting, "Crucify him! Crucify him!" Pilate addressed them a third time, "What evil has this man done? I found him guilty of no capital crime. Therefore I shall have him flogged and then release him." With loud shouts, however, they persisted in calling for his crucifixion, and their voices prevailed. The verdict of Pilate was that their demand should be granted. So he released the man who had been imprisoned for rebellion and murder, for whom they asked, and he handed Jesus over to them to deal with as they wished.

As they led him away they took hold of a certain Simon, a Cyrenian, who was coming in from the country; and after laying the cross on him, they made him carry it behind Jesus. A large crowd of people followed Jesus, including many women who mourned and lamented him.

Jesus turned to them and said, "Daughters of Jerusalem, do not weep for me; weep instead for yourselves and for your children for indeed, the days are coming when people will say, 'Blessed are the barren, the wombs that never bore and the breasts that never nursed.' At that time people will say to the mountains, 'Fall upon us!' and to the hills, 'Cover us!' for if these things are done when the wood is green, what will happen when it is dry?" Now two others, both criminals, were led away with him to be executed.

When they came to the place called the Skull, they crucified him and the criminals there, one on his right, the other on his left. Then Jesus said, "Father, forgive them, they know not what they do." They divided his garments by casting lots. The people stood by and watched; the rulers, meanwhile, sneered at him and said, "He saved others, let him save himself if he is the chosen one, the Christ of God." Even the soldiers jeered at him. As they approached to offer him wine they called out, "If you are King of the Jews, save yourself." Above him there was an inscription that read, "This is the King of the Jews."

Now one of the criminals hanging there reviled Jesus, saying, "Are you not the Christ? Save yourself and us." The other, however, rebuking him, said in reply, "Have you no fear of God, for you are subject to the same condemnation? And indeed, we have been condemned justly, for the sentence we received corresponds to our crimes, but this man has done nothing criminal." Then he said, "Jesus, remember me when you come into your kingdom." He replied to him, "Amen, I say to you, today you will be with me in Paradise."

It was now about noon and darkness came over the whole land until three in the afternoon because of an eclipse of the sun. Then the veil of the temple was torn down the middle. Jesus cried out in a loud voice, "Father, into your hands I commend my spirit"; and when he had said this he breathed his last.

Here all kneel and pause for a short time.

The centurion who witnessed what had happened glorified God and said, "This man was innocent beyond doubt." When all the people who had gathered for this spectacle saw what had happened, they returned home beating their breasts; but all his acquaintances stood at a distance, including the women who had followed him from Galilee and saw these events.

Now there was a virtuous and righteous man named Joseph, who, though he was a member of the council, had not consented to their plan of action. He came from the Jewish town of Arimathea and was awaiting the kingdom of God. He went to Pilate and asked for the body of Jesus. After he had taken the body down, he wrapped it in a linen cloth and laid him in a rock-hewn tomb in which no one had yet been buried. It was the day of preparation, and the sabbath was about to begin. The women who had come from Galilee with him followed behind, and when they had seen the tomb and the way in which his body was laid in it, they returned and prepared spices and perfumed oils. Then they rested on the sabbath according to the commandment.

LUKE 22: 14-71 & 23: 1-56

Shorter form: LUKE 23:1-49

ST. FRANCIS DE SALES

"It is at the foot of this cross that we should remain always. It is the place where the imitators of our Sovereign Master and Savior ordinarily abide. For it is from the cross that they receive the heavenly liqueur of holy charity. It streams out in great profusion from a divine Source, the bosom of our good God's divine mercy" (Lenten Sermons, *97*).

REFLECTION

"Let the world cry out as much as it wants; let human prudence censure and condemn our actions as much as it desires; we may have to listen to and suffer from all of this, but let us not be frightened or give up; let us rather pursue our course firmly and faithfully. Let worldly wisdom go on constituting what it considers excellence in worldly glory if it wants to. The true Christian, . . . who is tending toward Christian perfection, should, contrary to all the reasonings of human prudence, place all of his perfection in the folly of the cross [1 Cor. 1:18, 23], because it was in the folly of the cross that Our Lord was made perfect. So all the saints have endeavored to become wise in this folly, for this, they suffered all the contempt, censures and humiliations which came to them from the worldly wise. Perfection of the cross requires that we endure labors, persecutions and reprehensions for justice's sake. 'Blessed are those who are persecuted for justice' sake. [Mt. 5:10]. This wisdom is wholly contrary to that of the world. Even though Our Lord cried out again and again: 'Blessed are the poor in spirit, the peacemakers, the meek, they who hunger and thirst for justice [Mt. 5:3–6], the world cannot embrace this wisdom. It cries out: 'Oh! How blessed are the wealthy, the oppressors, those who take vengeance on their enemies, and those whom one dare not offend.' See how the perfection of the cross is folly in the eyes of the world precisely because it embraces what is abhorrent to human nature" (*Lenten Sermons*, 166–67).

PRAYER

Loving Father, give me the strength to persevere in my good resolutions and to disregard the remarks and unkind comments that others may make about my desire to love and serve you more faithfully. Teach me to understand and love the folly of the cross. Grant this through Christ Our Lord. Amen.

GOSPEL

Six days before Passover Jesus came to Bethany, where Lazarus was, whom Jesus had raised from the dead. They gave a dinner for him there, and Martha served, while Lazarus was one of those reclining at table with him. Mary took a liter of costly perfumed oil made from genuine aromatic nard and anointed the feet of Jesus and dried them with her hair; the house was filled with the fragrance of the oil. Then Judas the Iscariot, one of his disciples, and the one who would betray him, said, "Why was this oil not sold for three hundred days' wages and given to the poor?" He said this not because he cared about the poor but because he was a thief and held the money bag and used to steal the contributions. So Jesus said, "Leave her alone. Let her keep this for the day of my burial. You always have the poor with you, but you do not always have me."

The large crowd of the Jews found out that he was there and came, not only because of him, but also to see Lazarus, whom he had raised from the dead. And the chief priests plotted to kill Lazarus too, because many of the Jews were turning away and believing in Jesus because of him.

JOHN 12: 1-11

ST. FRANCIS DE SALES

"No one is ready ever to admit that he is avaricious. Everyone denies having so base and mean a heart. One man excuses himself that he has to take care of his children. . . . He never has enough; he always finds need for more" (IDL, pt. 3, ch. 14).

REFLECTION

"Judas and the evil rich man were avaricious . . . They were avid to amass riches, to obtain money and more money, but they also concealed and clung so strongly to the goods they had, and loved them excessively, that they adored them and made them their god. Holy Scripture speaks of them in this way: The avaricious man makes a god of his gold and silver [Eph. 5:5; Col. 3:51], and the voluptuous makes a god of his body [Phil. 3:19]. There is a great difference between drinking wine and becoming intoxicated, between using riches and adoring them. He who drinks wine out of necessity does no evil; but he who takes it to such an excess that he becomes intoxicated offends God mortally, loses his judgment, drowns his reason in the wine he drinks, and if he happens to die in this state, is damned. It is as if he said while drinking, 'If I die I wish to be lost and damned eternally.' There is a difference between using riches and adoring them. To use riches according to one's state and condition, when it is done as it should be, is permissible. But to make an idol of them is to be condemned and damned. In a word, there is a great difference between seeing and regarding the things of this world, and in wishing to enjoy them as if our happiness consisted in them. The first way is good, the last damnable" (*Lenten Sermons*, 74–75).

PRAYER

Help me, Lord, to appreciate the many gifts you have given me. Never let me be so caught up with material things that they stand in the way of serving you and sharing with those in need. Grant this in Jesus' name. Amen.

GOSPEL

Reclining at table with his disciples, Jesus was deeply troubled and testified, "Amen, amen, I say to you, one of you will betray me." The disciples looked at one another, at a loss as to whom he meant. One of his disciples, the one whom Jesus loved, was reclining at Jesus' side. So Simon Peter nodded to him to find out whom he meant. He leaned back against Jesus' chest and said to him, "Master, who is it?" Jesus answered, "It is the one to whom I hand the morsel after I have dipped it." So he dipped the morsel and took it and handed it to Judas, son of Simon the Iscariot. After Judas took the morsel, Satan entered him. So Jesus said to him, "What you are going to do, do quickly." Now none of those reclining at table realized why he said this to him. Some thought that since Judas kept the money bag, Jesus had told him, "Buy what we need for the feast," or to give something to the poor. So Judas took the morsel and left at once. And it was night.

When he had left, Jesus said, "Now is the Son of Man glorified, and God is glorified in him. If God is glorified in him, God will also glorify him in himself, and he will glorify him at once. My children, I will be with you only a little while longer. You will look for me, and as I told the Jews, 'Where I go you cannot come,' so now I say it to you."

Simon Peter said to him, "Master, where are you going?" Jesus answered him, "Where I am going, you cannot follow me now, though you will follow later." Peter said to him, "Master, why can I not follow you now? I will lay down my life for you." Jesus answered, "Will you lay down your life for me? Amen, amen, I say to you, the cock will not crow before you deny me three times."

JOHN 13: 21-33, 36-38

ST. FRANCIS DE SALES

"[There] are two kinds of sinners—which should make us live in great fear and trembling [Ps. 2:11; Phil. 2:12], but also in great hope and confidence, because of these two kinds, one was saved and one damned" (Lenten Sermons, *195).*

REFLECTION

"How fearful a thing it is to fall into the hands of the living God! [Heb. 10:31]. How inscrutable his judgments [Rm. 11:33]. Let anyone who is standing be fearful lest he fall, says the apostle [1 Cor. 10:12]; let no one glory in finding himself expressly called by God to a place where there seems to be nothing to fear. Let no one presume on his good works and think he has nothing more to fear. St. Peter, who had received so many graces, who had promised to accompany Our Lord to prison and even to death [Lk. 22:33], denied Him nevertheless at the whimpering taunt of a chambermaid. Judas sold him for such a small sum of money.

"These falls were both very great, but there was this difference. One acknowledged his guilt; the other despaired. Yet, our Savior had inspired in the heart of both the same *Peccavi* ('I have sinned'), that same *Peccavi* that God inspired in David's heart [2 Kings (2 Sam) 12:13]. Yes, he inspired it in both apostles, but one rejected it and the other accepted it. Hearing the cock crow, St. Peter remembered what he had done and the word his good Master had spoken to him. Then, acknowledging his sin, he went out and wept bitterly [Mt. 26:74–75; Lk. 22:61–62] that he received what we today call a plenary indulgence and full remission of all his sins. O happy St. Peter! By such contrition for your sins you received a full pardon for such great disloyalty!

"On the other hand, although Judas received this same inspiration for the same *Peccavi*, he rejected it and despaired . . . This *Peccavi* sent to the heart of Judas was truly like that sent to David. Why then was Judas not converted? O miserable man! He saw the gravity of his crime and despaired. Truly, he confessed his sin, for in returning to the chief priests the thirty pieces of silver for which he had sold his Master, he acknowledged aloud that he had sold innocent blood [Mt. 27:3–5]. But these priests would give him no absolution. Alas, did not this unhappy man know that Our Lord alone could give it to him, that he was the Savior and held Redemption in His Hands?" (*Lenten Sermons*, 192–94).

PRAYER

May I, like Peter, Lord, recognize and readily acknowledge my sins by honestly and humbly confessing them and express my eternal gratitude for your merciful forgiveness. Grant this in Jesus' name. Amen.

GOSPEL

One of the Twelve, who was called Judas Iscariot, went to the chief priests and said, "What are you willing to give me if I hand him over to you?" They paid him thirty pieces of silver, and from that time on he looked for an opportunity to hand him over.

On the first day of the Feast of Unleavened Bread, the disciples approached Jesus and said, "Where do you want us to prepare for you to eat the Passover?" He said, "Go into the city to a certain man and tell him, 'The teacher says, "My appointed time draws near; in your house I shall celebrate the Passover with my disciples."'" The disciples then did as Jesus had ordered, and prepared the Passover.

When it was evening, he reclined at table with the Twelve. And while they were eating, he said, "Amen, I say to you, one of you will betray me." Deeply distressed at this, they began to say to him one after another, "Surely it is not I, Lord?" He said in reply, "He who has dipped his hand into the dish with me is the one who will betray me. The Son of Man indeed goes, as it is written of him, but woe to that man by whom the Son of Man is betrayed. It would be better for that man if he had never been born." Then Judas, his betrayer, said in reply, "Surely it is not I, Rabbi?" He answered, "You have said so."

MATTHEW 26: 14-25

ST. FRANCIS DE SALES

"Avarice is a raging fever that makes itself all the harder to detect the more violent and burning it is" (IDL, pt. 3, ch. 14).

215

REFLECTION

"Judas . . . miserably sold his Master, and at so vile a price [Mt. 26:15] . . . How terrible and appalling are the falls of God's servants, especially those who have received great graces. What greater grace could there be than that given to St. Peter and Judas? Like Peter, Judas too had been called to be an apostle by Our Lord Himself, who preferred him to so many millions of others who would have done great marvels in this ministry. The Savior bestowed special favors upon him. Besides giving him the gift of miracles, he also foretold him his betrayal [Mt. 26:21–25; Jn. 12:18–27], so that being forewarned he might avoid it. Knowing that he was attracted to dealing with and managing affairs [Jn. 12:6; 13:29], he made him procurator of his sacred college. He did this to gain his heart entirely and to omit nothing that could render him more devoted to his Divine Majesty. Nevertheless, this miserable Judas abused all these graces and sold his good Master.

"How frightful and dangerous are the falls from the mountains! As soon as one begins to fall, one rolls inexorably to the very bottom of the precipice. Such has been the falls of several who fell away from the service of God. Frightening, indeed, that after a good beginning even after having lived thirty or forty years in this holy service, in old age, when it is time to reap, one flings himself into the abyss and loses all. Such was the misfortune of Solomon, whose salvation is very doubtful, and of several others who deserted the right path in their last years" (*Lenten Sermons*, 191–92).

PRAYER

Father, my sinful betrayals become all the more evident and loathsome to me when I contemplate the innumerable gifts and kindnesses you daily and lovingly bestow on me. During this most holy of all weeks, may my gratitude grow and increase so as to keep me firmly on the path that is most pleasing to you. Grant this in Jesus' name. Amen.

QUESTIONS FOR REFLECTION
OR DISCUSSION

1. How does St. Francis de Sales help us to have that same mind and attitude as Jesus as we get closer to celebrating his Passion, death and resurrection?

2. In what ways are we inclined to trust in our own resources rather than in God's favor and inspirations?

3. In view of our sinfulness, how does St. Francis de Sales encourage us not to become discouraged?

4. How do we look upon the nature of sin and our relationship with the Lord and with others?

5. How does the folly of the Cross affect my daily life and dealings?

PASCHAL
TRIDUUM

GOSPEL

Jesus came to Nazareth, where he had grown up, and went according to his custom into the synagogue on the sabbath day. He stood up to read and was handed a scroll of the prophet Isaiah. He unrolled the scroll and found the passage where it was written:

The Spirit of the Lord is upon me,
because he has anointed me
*   to bring glad tidings to the poor.*
He has sent me to proclaim liberty to captives
*   and recovery of sight to the blind,*
*   to let the oppressed go free,*
and to proclaim a year acceptable to the Lord.

Rolling up the scroll, he handed it back to the attendant and sat down, and the eyes of all in the synagogue looked intently at him. He said to them, "Today this Scripture passage is fulfilled in your hearing."

LUKE 4: 16-21

ST. FRANCIS DE SALES

"Let us be what we are and be that well, in order to bring honor to the Master Craftsman whose handiwork we are . . . Let us be what God wants us to be, provided we are his, and let us not be what we would like to be contrary to his intention" (Letters of Spiritual Direction, *111).*

REFLECTION

As we enter the three most holy days of Lent, we learn how Jesus came to a deeper understanding of himself and of the mission his Father gave him. The ease and facility with which he opened the scroll of the

† The Chrism Mass is the annual Mass when the bishop blesses the oils that will be used for the sacraments throughout the year in the diocese.

scriptures and went directly to the passage he desired to read indicates a great familiarity with God's Word which undoubtedly shaped the image he had of himself. Of course, Jesus was anointed from all eternity by the Holy Spirit in the sense of his coming forth from the Father generated the Holy Spirit, the bond of eternal love between them. He understood his being sent by the Father to heal and redeem us as an anointing or being set aside by the Father for this task of reconciliation. Being anointed by the Holy Spirit essentially means being set aside or consecrated by love for love. Our saint understood love as a dynamic and creative power that involves the movement of our heart or will to seek and pursue whatever is truly good. So Jesus understands himself as being sent by the Father to perform what our saint calls the ecstasy of good works. These are enumerated in the scriptural passage Jesus read and defines the nature and mission of the Messiah, the Anointed One. This reaching out to heal, console, encourage and support connects and unites Jesus with those in need, that is, with all of humanity which, since the fall, is born in what our saint calls great "indigence" (TLG, 1:91:92).

So anointing by the Holy Spirit, by Holy Love, motivates Jesus and causes us to be united and joined to him and to each other in a bond of holy communion. Since we are all anointed by the Holy Spirit in our baptism and made to share in the priestly ministry of Jesus, we are all called to collaborate with him in completing both the work of creation and redemption. "God," he says, "could have created us in paradise and placed us there from our childhood. Our nature, however, requires that he make us his collaborators." To add greater strength to his argument, he quotes St. Augustine: "He who made us without us, does not save us without us" (*OEA*, 7:13–14).

PRAYER

Dear Lord, help me to accept and love myself as you accept and love me. May I become ever more conscious of my sacred anointing so that like Jesus I may generously, lovingly and perseveringly reach out to those in need to bring encouragement, healing, true freedom, and peace. I ask this in Jesus' name. Amen.

GOSPEL

Before the feast of Passover, Jesus knew that his hour had come to pass from this world to the Father. He loved his own in the world and he loved them to the end. The devil had already induced Judas, son of Simon the Iscariot, to hand him over. So, during supper, fully aware that the Father had put everything into his power and that he had come from God and was returning to God, he rose from supper and took off his outer garments. He took a towel and tied it around his waist. Then he poured water into a basin and began to wash the disciples' feet and dry them with the towel around his waist. He came to Simon Peter, who said to him, "Master, are you going to wash my feet?" Jesus answered and said to him, "What I am doing, you do not understand now, but you will understand later." Peter said to him, "You will never wash my feet." Jesus answered him, "Unless I wash you, you will have no inheritance with me." Simon Peter said to him, "Master, then not only my feet, but my hands and head as well." Jesus said to him, "Whoever has bathed has no need except to have his feet washed, for he is clean all over; so you are clean, but not all." For he knew who would betray him; for this reason, he said, "Not all of you are clean."

So when he had washed their feet and put his garments back on and reclined at table again, he said to them, "Do you realize what I have done for you? You call me 'teacher' and 'master,' and rightly so, for indeed I am. If I, therefore, the master and teacher, have washed your feet, you ought to wash one another's feet. I have given you a model to follow, so that as I have done for you, you should also do."

JOHN 13: 1-15

ST. FRANCIS DE SALES

"All spiritual doctors agree on what are the two things principally necessary for the reception of Communion, namely, the proper disposition of the soul and the right desire. However, since the right desire is part of the proper disposition of soul, we can say that only one thing is required, namely, the proper disposition of the soul. Let us then see how we are to place our souls in the proper disposition, in so far as this is possible, in order to worthily receive Communion" (OEA, 26:211).

REFLECTION

"With regard to the will, we must . . . cleanse it from one thing and adorn it with another. We must cleanse it of disordered and inordinate affections, even of good things. This is why those who ate the paschal lamb had to have their feet shod [Ex. 12:11] so that they would not touch the ground with their feet for 'the feet are the affections of the soul' which carry it wherever it goes, says St. Augustine [*Enarrt*. In Ps. 94:2]. These affections must not touch the ground nor given free rein but must be restrained and checked when eating the true Paschal Lamb, which is the Most Holy Sacrament. Thus Our Lord washed the feet of his apostles before instituting it [Jn. 13:5–9] to show that the affections of communicants must be very pure.

"The manna had to be gathered early in the morning before the sun came up because the natural warm breezes, that is, the inordinate affections for children, parents, friends, material things, and comforts prevent us from gathering this heavenly food. We have to approach it with a fresh soul and will, not one impassioned nor smitten by any other thing except the gathering of this manna. But we have to adorn it with the will of an affection and extreme desire for this heavenly food, for this hidden manna. This is why those who ate the paschal lamb were commanded to do so eagerly and quickly [Ex. 12] and those who gathered it to get up very early [Ex. 16:21]. Our Lord himself, before instituting this holy sacrament, greatly desired it: 'I have desired,' he said, 'with a great desire to eat this Passover meal with you' [Lk. 22:15]. The soul, being disposed in this fashion in its three principal faculties, bears admirable fruit in Holy Communion" (*OEA*, 26:215).

PRAYER

What an incomprehensible gesture of love and service, merciful Father, your son Jesus has given us by washing the feet of his disciples and commanding us to do the same! May our worthy reception of the Bread of Life incline us to generously render humble service to one another. We ask this in Jesus' name. Amen.

GOSPEL

Jesus went out with his disciples across the Kidron valley to where there was a garden, into which he and his disciples entered. Judas his betrayer also knew the place, because Jesus had often met there with his disciples. So Judas got a band of soldiers and guards from the chief priests and the Pharisees and went there with lanterns, torches, and weapons. Jesus, knowing everything that was going to happen to him, went out and said to them, "Whom are you looking for?" They answered him, "Jesus the Nazorean." He said to them, "I AM." Judas his betrayer was also with them. When he said to them, "I AM," they turned away and fell to the ground. So he again asked them, "Whom are you looking for?" They said, "Jesus the Nazorean." Jesus answered, "I told you that I AM. So if you are looking for me, let these men go." This was to fulfill what he had said, "I have not lost any of those you gave me." Then Simon Peter, who had a sword, drew it, struck the high priest's slave, and cut off his right ear. The slave's name was Malchus. Jesus said to Peter, "Put your sword into its scabbard. Shall I not drink the cup that the Father gave me?"

So the band of soldiers, the tribune, and the Jewish guards seized Jesus, bound him, and brought him to Annas first. He was the father-in-law of Caiaphas, who was high priest that year. It was Caiaphas who had counseled the Jews that it was better that one man should die rather than the people.

Simon Peter and another disciple followed Jesus. Now the other disciple was known to the high priest, and he entered the courtyard of the high priest with Jesus. But Peter stood at the gate outside. So the other disciple, the acquaintance of the high priest, went out and spoke to the gatekeeper and brought Peter in. Then the maid who was the gatekeeper said to Peter, "You are not one of this man's disciples, are you?" He said, "I am not." Now the slaves and the guards were standing around a charcoal fire that they had made, because it was cold, and were warming themselves. Peter was also standing there keeping warm.

The high priest questioned Jesus about his disciples and about his doctrine. Jesus answered him, "I have spoken publicly to the world. I have always taught in a synagogue or in the temple area where all the Jews gather, and in secret I have said nothing. Why ask me? Ask those who heard me what I said to them. They know what I said." When he had said this, one of the temple guards standing there struck Jesus and said, "Is this the way you answer the high priest?" Jesus answered him, "If I have spoken wrongly, testify to the wrong; but if I have spoken rightly, why do you strike me?" Then Annas sent him bound to Caiaphas the high priest.

Now Simon Peter was standing there keeping warm. And they said to him, "You are not one of his disciples, are you?" He denied it and said, "I am not." One of the slaves of the high priest, a relative of the one whose ear Peter had cut off, said, "Didn't I see you in the garden with him?" Again Peter denied it. And immediately the cock crowed.

Then they brought Jesus from Caiaphas to the praetorium. It was morning. And they themselves did not enter the praetorium, in order not to be defiled so that they could eat the Passover. So Pilate came out to them and said, "What charge do you bring against this man?" They answered and said to him, "If he were not a criminal, we would not have handed him over to you." At this, Pilate said to them, "Take him yourselves, and judge him according to your law." The Jews answered him, "We do not have the right to execute anyone," in order that the word of Jesus might be fulfilled that he said indicating the kind of death he would die.

So Pilate went back into the praetorium and summoned Jesus and said to him, "Are you the King of the Jews?" Jesus answered, "Do you say this on your own or have others told you about me?" Pilate answered, "I am not a Jew, am I? Your own nation and the chief priests handed you over to me. What have you done?" Jesus answered, "My kingdom does not belong to this world. If my kingdom did belong to this world, my attendants would be fighting to keep me from being handed over to the Jews. But as it is, my kingdom is not here." So Pilate said to him, "Then you are a king?" Jesus answered, "You say I am a king. For this I was born and for this I came into the world, to testify to the truth. Everyone who belongs to the truth listens to my voice." Pilate said to him, "What is truth?"

When he had said this, he again went out to the Jews and said to them, "I find no guilt in him. But you have a custom that I release one prisoner to you at Passover. Do you want me to release to you the King of the Jews?" They cried out again, "Not this one but Barabbas!" Now Barabbas was a revolutionary.

Then Pilate took Jesus and had him scourged. And the soldiers wove a crown out of thorns and placed it on his head, and clothed him in a purple cloak, and they came to him and said, "Hail, King of the Jews!" And they struck him repeatedly. Once more Pilate went out and said to them, "Look, I am bringing him out to you, so that you may know that I find no guilt in him." So Jesus came out, wearing the crown of thorns and the purple cloak. And he said to them, "Behold, the man!" When the chief priests and the guards saw him they cried out, "Crucify him, crucify him!" Pilate said to them, "Take him yourselves and crucify him. I find no guilt in him." The Jews answered, "We have a law, and according to that law he ought to die, because he made himself the Son of God." Now when Pilate heard this statement, he became even more afraid, and went back into the praetorium and said to Jesus, "Where are you from?" Jesus did not answer him. So Pilate said to him, "Do you not speak to me? Do you not know that I have power to release you and I have power to crucify you?" Jesus answered him, "You would have no power over me if it had not been given to you from above. For this reason the one who handed me over to you has the greater sin." Consequently, Pilate tried to release him;

but the Jews cried out, "If you release him, you are not a Friend of Caesar. Everyone who makes himself a king opposes Caesar."

When Pilate heard these words he brought Jesus out and seated him on the judge's bench in the place called Stone Pavement, in Hebrew, Gabbatha. It was preparation day for Passover, and it was about noon. And he said to the Jews, "Behold, your king!" They cried out, "Take him away, take him away! Crucify him!" Pilate said to them, "Shall I crucify your king?" The chief priests answered, "We have no king but Caesar." Then he handed him over to them to be crucified.

So they took Jesus, and, carrying the cross himself, he went out to what is called the Place of the Skull, in Hebrew, Golgotha. There they crucified him, and with him two others, one on either side, with Jesus in the middle. Pilate also had an inscription written and put on the cross. It read, "Jesus the Nazorean, the King of the Jews." Now many of the Jews read this inscription, because the place where Jesus was crucified was near the city; and it was written in Hebrew, Latin, and Greek. So the chief priests of the Jews said to Pilate, "Do not write 'The King of the Jews,' but that he said, 'I am the King of the Jews'." Pilate answered, "What I have written, I have written."

When the soldiers had crucified Jesus, they took his clothes and divided them into four shares, a share for each soldier. They also took his tunic, but the tunic was seamless, woven in one piece from the top down. So they said to one another, "Let's not tear it, but cast lots for it to see whose it will be," in order that the passage of Scripture might be fulfilled that says:

They divided my garments among them,
and for my vesture they cast lots.

This is what the soldiers did. Standing by the cross of Jesus were his mother and his mother's sister, Mary the wife of Clopas, and Mary of Magdala. When Jesus saw his mother and the disciple there whom he loved he said to his mother, "Woman, behold, your son." Then he said to the disciple, "Behold, your mother." And from that hour the disciple took her into his home.

After this, aware that everything was now finished, in order that the Scripture might be fulfilled, Jesus said, "I thirst." There was a vessel filled with common wine. So they put a sponge soaked in wine on a sprig of hyssop and put it up to his mouth. When Jesus had taken the wine, he said, "It is finished." And bowing his head, he handed over the spirit.

Here all kneel and pause for a short time.

Now since it was preparation day, in order that the bodies might not remain on the cross on the sabbath, for the sabbath day of that week was a solemn one, the Jews asked Pilate that their legs be broken and that they be taken down. So the soldiers came and broke the legs of the first and then of the other one who was crucified with Jesus. But when they came to Jesus and saw that he was already dead, they did not break his legs, but one soldier thrust his lance into his side, and immediately blood and water flowed out. An eyewitness has testified, and his testimony is true; he knows that he is speaking the truth, so that you also may come to believe. For this happened so that the Scripture passage might be fulfilled: *Not a bone of it will be broken.* And again another passage says: *They will look upon him whom they have pierced.*

After this, Joseph of Arimathea, secretly a disciple of Jesus for fear of the Jews, asked Pilate if he could remove the body of Jesus. And Pilate permitted it. So he came and took his body. Nicodemus, the one who had first come to him at night, also came bringing a mixture of myrrh and aloes weighing about one hundred pounds. They took the body of Jesus and bound it with burial cloths along with the spices, according to the Jewish burial custom. Now in the place where he had been crucified there was a garden, and in the garden a new tomb, in which no one had yet been buried. So they laid Jesus there because of the Jewish preparation day; for the tomb was close by.

JOHN 18: 1-40 & 19: 1-42

ST. FRANCIS DE SALES

"Upon Calvary we cannot have life without love, or love without the Redeemer's death. Except there, all is either eternal death or eternal love. All Christian wisdom consists in choosing rightly" (TLG, II:281).

REFLECTION

Our saint recounts the story of a very virtuous knight who visits the holy places of Palestine and in particular those associated with Jesus' Passion and death. These can serve as a fruitful reflection for prayer: "He seems to see once again Our Lord on his knees in the Cenacle, washing the feet of his disciples and later distributing to them his own divine body in the Holy Eucharist. He passes the brook of Cedron and goes on to the garden of Gethesemani where his heart melts in tears of most loving sorrow while in that place he represents to himself his dear Savior sweating blood and the bitter agony he suffered there soon afterwards tied, haltered and led into Jerusalem. He takes that same path and follows everywhere the footprints of his beloved. In imagination he sees him dragged here and there to Annas, to Caiphas, to Pilate, to Herod. He sees Christ scourged, blindfolded, spat upon, crowned with thorns, shown to the people, condemned to death, and loaded with his cross which he carries, and as he carries it he has a pitiable meeting with his Mother, plunged deep in grief and with the daughters of Jerusalem who weep over him.

"At last this devout pilgrim climbs up Mount Calvary, where in spirit he sees the cross laid down upon the earth, and Our Lord, stripped naked, thrown down, and most cruelly nailed hand and foot upon it. He then contemplates how they raise the cross and the Crucified into the air, and he sees the blood that rushed down from all parts of the divine body that hung there. He regards the poor Holy Virgin, pierced through and through with the sword of sorrow. At last he sees Christ dying, then dead, then receiving the stroke of the lance and showing through the open wound his divine heart, then taken down from the cross and carried to the sepulcher. He follows him there, shedding a sea of tears on the places wet with the Redeemer's blood. He enters the tomb and buries his heart with the body of his Master" (*TLG*, II:45–46).

PRAYER

"Oh! Lord Jesus, I beg you, pierce my heart with your divine wounds, inebriate me with your blood so that in this supernatural inebriation, in whatever direction I turn, I will see you always crucified and that everything appear to my eyes red with your blood in such a way that, uniquely occupied with you, may I find nothing but you, may I consider nothing but your sacred wounds" (*OEA*, 8:429). Amen.

GOSPEL

After the sabbath, as the first day of the week was dawning, Mary Magdalene and the other Mary came to see the tomb. And behold, there was a great earthquake; for an angel of the Lord descended from heaven, approached, rolled back the stone, and sat upon it. His appearance was like lightning and his clothing was white as snow. The guards were shaken with fear of him and became like dead men. Then the angel said to the women in reply, "Do not be afraid! I know that you are seeking Jesus the crucified. He is not here, for he has been raised just as he said. Come and see the place where he lay. Then go quickly and tell his disciples, 'He has been raised from the dead, and he is going before you to Galilee; there you will see him.' Behold, I have told you." Then they went away quickly from the tomb, fearful yet overjoyed, and ran to announce this to his disciples. And behold, Jesus met them on their way and greeted them. They approached, embraced his feet, and did him homage. Then Jesus said to them, "Do not be afraid. Go tell my brothers to go to Galilee, and there they will see me."

MATTHEW 28: 1-10

ST. FRANCIS DE SALES

"We must strip ourselves of all affections both little and great, make a frequent examination of our heart to see if it is truly ready to divest itself of all its garments as Isaiah did. Then at the proper time, we must take up again the affections suitable to the service of charity, so that we may die naked upon the cross with our divine Savior and afterwards rise again with him in the new man [Rm. 6:4–6]. 'Love is as strong as death' [Cant. 8:5] to enable us to forsake all things. It is as magnificent as the resurrection to adorn us with glory and honor" (TLG, II:139–40).

REFLECTION

"If the sky, the air and the earth and everything in them seem to be rejuvenated and as if rising from death to life in this sweet season of spring, dear listeners, very dear and cherished Christian souls, they are rewarded by the works of the Savior and Lord, since the sky remained so long a time somber and dark, appears to be dressed in the most beautiful and most bright robe; the air, a little while ago, all full of cold and dampness, with fog and melancholy clouds discovers itself now to be so pure, so calm, so well in harmony with the season; the earth devastated by the rigors of winter, appears now all dappled with its verdant and blossoming coating.

"If the Church, our Mother, which has been austere, wearing only gloomy habits, chanting only lamentations, showing only a sad and aggrieved countenance, in mourning the death of her Spouse, but now, as if to renew its marriage to the same resurrected Lord and Spouse, has well-appointed and adorned the best it can all of its houses, continues to hold joyful and uplifting ceremonies, chants only hymns of jubilation and consolation; if dark hell had even been changed into brightness by the luminous countenance of Our Lord who descended there; if the angels appeared with their robes whiter than usual [Mt. 28:3], shall we, O Christians, among all creatures remain dead and unaffected in our unattractiveness and sadness? Why don't we put on our new beautiful clothing? But I would like to see us also change just as the season changes, but not in the same way. The serenity of the sky and of the air, this attractiveness of the earth does not perdure. It is subject to inconstancy . . . We need to adorn ourselves after the example of another patron and model, after the model of the resurrection of Our Lord: 'As Christ is risen from the dead, so let us walk in newness of" the spirit [Rm. 5:4]. Our Savior, like an eagle, has now changed his feathers and has clothed himself with strength and glory [Ps. 92:1]" (*OEA*, 10:431–33).

PRAYER

Dear Lord, may the resurrection of Jesus, deeply affect my life and my actions so that I will rejoice in the newness of life he has bestowed on me by keeping my life in complete harmony with his. Grant this in Jesus' name. Amen.

GOSPEL

When the sabbath was over, Mary Magdalene, Mary, the mother of James, and Salome bought spices so that they might go and anoint him. Very early when the sun had risen, on the first day of the week, they came to the tomb. They were saying to one another, "Who will roll back the stone for us from the entrance to the tomb?" When they looked up, they saw that the stone had been rolled back; it was very large. On entering the tomb they saw a young man sitting on the right side, clothed in a white robe, and they were utterly amazed. He said to them, "Do not be amazed! You seek Jesus of Nazareth, the crucified. He has been raised; he is not here. Behold the place where they laid him. "But go and tell his disciples and Peter, 'He is going before you to Galilee; there you will see him, as he told you.'"

MARK 16: 1-7

ST. FRANCIS DE SALES

"Oppose vigorously any tendency to sadness. Although it may seem that all that you do at this time is done coldly, sadly, and sluggishly, you must nevertheless persevere . . . Perform fervent external actions, even though you may perform them without relish, such as embracing a crucifix, clasping it to your breast, kissing the feet and the hands, lifting up your eyes and your hands to heaven, raising your voice to God in words of love and confidence" (IDL, pt. 4, ch.12).

REFLECTION

The dejection and the sadness that the women who went to the tomb experienced was, no doubt, very profound. This experience figures in the reflection that our saint makes on the nature of evil and good sadness. "Evil sadness loses heart, becomes listless and sits back, causing us to abandon care and our work . . . Good sadness gives strength and courage, does not give up, nor abandon a good intention. It is like the sadness of Our Lord, even though it was great and unequalled, it did not stop him from praying for and looking after his apostles [Mt. 26:38; Jn. 18:8]. And Our Lady, having lost her son was very sad, but she did not stop looking diligently for him [Lk. 2:41; Jn. 20:1], as did also Mary Magdalene, without stopping to lament and cry uselessly.

"Evil sadness darkens the intellect, deprives the soul of counsel, of resolve and of judgment . . . Good sadness opens the mind, making it clear and lucid . . . Evil sadness inhibits prayer, makes it distasteful to us, and causes us lose confidence in God's goodness. In contradistinction, good sadness is from God, gives reassurance, increases our confidence in God, causes us to pray for and implore his mercy . . . In a word, those who are overcome with evil sadness experience a whole host of horrors, of errors, of useless fears, of trials and of fears of being abandoned by God and of being in his disfavor . . . But good sadness reasons in this way: 'I am a miserable, vile and abject creature, and yet, God exercises his mercy on me' . . . The basis for these differences between evil and good sadness is the Holy Spirit, who is the author of good sadness since he is the unique Consoler" (*OEA*, 26:229–30).

PRAYER

Merciful Lord, as you turned the sadness of the women at the tomb into supreme joy, teach us how the resurrection of Jesus can make us rise above the sad and sorrowful events of our life and enjoy here and in eternity the joy and peace of your Holy Spirit. We ask this in the name of Jesus, who rose triumphantly from the dead. Amen.

GOSPEL

At daybreak on the first day of the week the women who had come from Galilee with Jesus took the spices they had prepared and went to the tomb. They found the stone rolled away from the tomb; but when they entered, they did not find the body of the Lord Jesus. While they were puzzling over this, behold, two men in dazzling garments appeared to them. They were terrified and bowed their faces to the ground. They said to them, "Why do you seek the living one among the dead? He is not here, but he has been raised. Remember what he said to you while he was still in Galilee, that the Son of Man must be handed over to sinners and be crucified, and rise on the third day." And they remembered his words. Then they returned from the tomb and announced all these things to the eleven and to all others. The women were Mary Magdalene, Joanna, and Mary the mother of James; the others who accompanied them also told this to the apostles, but their story seemed like nonsense and they did not believe them. But Peter got up and ran to the tomb, bent down, and saw the burial cloths alone; then he went home amazed at what had happened.

LUKE 24: 1-12

ST. FRANCIS DE SALES

"The soul pours itself out by pleasures, and their diversity dissipates it and hinders it from being able to apply itself attentively to the pleasure it should take in God. A true lover has almost no other pleasure aside from the loved object" (TLG, I:251).

REFLECTION

It is the person of Mary Magdalene that captures the imagination of our saint in the Gospel narratives of the resurrection. She is the one whom our saint believes helps us focus our attention and our deepest longings on Jesus himself. "Certainly, not only are earthly things incapable of satisfying our hearts but also heavenly things. We see this very clearly in Mary Magdalene. The poor saint, all smitten with love for her Master, returned to look for him...after he died and was placed in the tomb. But not having found him but only angels, she was not contented with them even though they were very beautiful and dressed in an angelic fashion . . .

"Mary Magdalene does not find pleasure to be around these celestial spirits, neither in the beauty of their countenances nor in the whiteness of their robes, still less in their regal bearing. She goes and looks all around them, and they ask her: 'Woman, why are you crying? And what are you looking for?' 'They have taken away my Master,' she responds, 'and I do not know where they have placed him.' 'Why are you crying?' as if to say: 'Don't you have sufficient reason to rejoice and dry your tears on seeing us. Isn't the splendor and the beauty of our faces, the brightness of our clothing, our magnificence more grand than that of Solomon, enough to assuage your tears?' Certainly not, my heart can only be content in God. Mary Magdalene preferred her crucified Master to the glorified angels" (*OEA*, 9:171–72).

PRAYER

May we, dear Jesus, focus our deepest longings like St. Mary Magdalene on you alone. Let us not waste and dissipate our love on things that are not worthy of you. May it please you to grant this. Amen.

EASTER
SUNDAY

GOSPEL

On the first day of the week, Mary of Magdala came to the tomb early in the morning, while it was still dark, and saw the stone removed from the tomb. So she ran and went to Simon Peter and to the other disciple whom Jesus loved, and told them, "They have taken the Lord from the tomb, and we don't know where they put him." So Peter and the other disciple went out and came to the tomb. They both ran, but the other disciple ran faster than Peter and arrived at the tomb first; he bent down and saw the burial cloths there, but did not go in. When Simon Peter arrived after him, he went into the tomb and saw the burial cloths there, and the cloth that had covered his head, not with the burial cloths but rolled up in a separate place. Then the other disciple also went in, the one who had arrived at the tomb first, and he saw and believed. For they did not yet understand the Scripture that he had to rise from the dead.

JOHN 20: 1-9

Alternative readings from Easter Vigil or LUKE 24:13-35
at an afternoon or evening Mass.

ST. FRANCIS DE SALES

"Everything done out of love is love; work and even death is only love when we accept them out of love" (OEA, 15:101).

REFLECTION

The resurrection of Jesus was a great mystery and puzzle to the early disciples. This is revealed by the final words of today's Gospel: "For as yet they did not understand the Scripture that he had to rise from the dead" (Jn 20:9). The same thing can be said of all of us, namely, that we do not fully understand and appreciate what Christ's rising from the dead really means for us and for all of humanity. If Jesus' resurrection means anything, it means that it is God's protest against death and it is love that overcomes death. Pope Benedict XVI expresses it in this way: "Jesus Christ shows us how the truth of love can transform the dark mystery of death into the radiant light of the resurrection" (*Sacramentum caritatis*, 35). Love and resurrection go hand in hand. It was possible for Christ to pass over from death to life because of his love for us and for his Father. As John reminds us in one of his epistles: "We know that we have passed [passed over] from death to life [namely, have experienced the resurrection] because we love [others]" (1 Jn 3:14). Paraphrasing what he says elsewhere. "The one who does not love does not live." And the poet Emily Dickinson emphasized this truth when she wrote: "Love is the Fellow of the Resurrection scooping up the dust and chanting: 'Live" ("While It Is Alive").

For us Easter people, to live is to love and to live is to give witness to this love. What we and the world desperately need are people who are willing to witness not to the past but to the present, because like Peter we can say that we ate and drank with the Lord after he rose from the dead. We do this every time we partake of the Eucharistic meal where it is the resurrected body of Christ that is made present. We need to be an Easter people who have experienced a resurrection in our own lives, a people who can assure the world that death does not have the last word, that we have died to our sinful selves and now live the resurrected life of Jesus. That is the message, the good news that the world and the suffering millions expect from us.

Others can only learn of the resurrection of Christ through us, by the way we live and love. The only face that Christ can show to others today to convince and to convert them is our own, that of our Christian communities. "Where two or three are gathered in my name, there I am in the midst of them" (Mt 18:20). So the resurrected Christ promised to be with us when we come together in his name. We are the ones then who have to demonstrate the resurrection of Christ; we are the witnesses that Christ has risen and is alive in our midst. It is in this way, that we will come to understand what rising from the dead truly means.

PRAYER

Dear Jesus, having made this Lenten journey with you and your servant Francis de Sales, may you deepen my understanding of the mystery of your rising from the dead and what it means for me to lead a new life full of love for you and for others. May it please you to grant this. Amen.

EPILOGUE

Long journeys can both exhaust and exhilarate us, depending on what we decide to dwell on. After making an eagerly awaited trip, we generally want to share our experiences and especially the highlights with family and friends. To jog our memories and to better communicate what we have experienced, we generally take numerous photos and buy postcards and souvenirs. The nature of a spiritual journey closely parallels the normal trips we take for leisure and relaxation. As we try to relive this Lenten journey, we should prayerfully give thanks for all of the many graces and insights that we have received. As we turn these over in our minds, we should ask ourselves what were our most striking, our most vivid, our most lasting impressions. May I suggest that our special travel companion, St. Francis de Sales, has shown us how essential it is for us to pursue a deep spiritual life, which he calls the devout life, in order to make us more human and more closely resemble the Lord Jesus.

Our saint's insistence on beginning with our heart and our interior is central to the way he approaches the spiritual life because it is the only way in which we can truly change and improve our lives for the better. Through prayer, especially spiritual aspirations said very frequently throughout the day, we engrave Jesus in our hearts and once we have him in our hearts then he will come alive in all of our actions, both significant and insignificant. This is for the saint essentially a

Passover experience where, through Christ's Passover, we pass over from the more superficial layers of our consciousness to where faith, hope and charity dwell, what he refers to as our heart or the Holy of Holies when he compares our souls to the temple of Jerusalem. To become familiar with the state of our soul, our saint urges us to frequently examine what we love, that is, our hearts to see if they are in the right place. This is realized by frequent and daily reflections on God's word in Sacred Scripture and from any other source it may please the Lord to send it to us.

One of the things that should have impressed us in our Lenten journey is how balanced, yes, and even human, the saint's spirituality is. As we noted, Elisabeth Stopp characterized it as "inspired common sense." St. Francis believed that we should do all things in moderation except loving God. He advises us to admire but not imitate the sometimes bizarre and extremely demanding austerities of a number of the saints. He shows us numerous ways of how the spiritual life can be readily adapted to all walks of life, inside and outside of the cloister or the clerical state. One of the primary means he proposes to achieve this is through the frequent practice of the Direction of Intention throughout the day, by performing all of our actions no matter how small out of love for God. This practice counteracts the maxim: "Hell is filled with good intentions" by showing us how "Heaven is filled with good intentions."

Our saint stresses the compatibility and adaptability of the spiritual life or devotion to all walks of life: "Every devotion becomes agreeable when united with devotion. Care of one's family is rendered more peaceable, love of husband and wife more sincere, service to one's prince more faithful, and every type of employment more pleasant and agreeable" (*IDL*, pt. 1, ch. 3). By the way we live our spiritual or devout life, we must make it attractive and lovable to others so that they will be enticed to make their own personal journey with Jesus and St. Francis de Sales.

APPENDIX A:
CALENDAR OF LENT 2011–2020
& LECTIONARY CYCLE

Ash Wednesday–Easter

Year	Sunday Year	Lent	Date
2011	A	Ash Wednesday	March 9
		1st Sunday of Lent	March 13
		2nd Sunday of Lent	March 20
		3rd Sunday of Lent	March 27
		4th Sunday of Lent	April 3
		5th Sunday of Lent	April 10
		Palm Sunday	April 17
		Paschal Triduum	April 21
		Easter Sunday	April 24
2012	B	Ash Wednesday	February 22
		1st Sunday of Lent	February 26
		2nd Sunday of Lent	March 4
		3rd Sunday of Lent	March 11
		4th Sunday of Lent	March 18
		5th Sunday of Lent	March 25
		Palm Sunday	April 1
		Paschal Triduum	April 5
		Easter Sunday	April 8

Year	Sunday Year	Lent	Date
2013	C	Ash Wednesday	February 13
		1st Sunday of Lent	February 17
		2nd Sunday of Lent	February 24
		3rd Sunday of Lent	March 3
		4th Sunday of Lent	March 10
		5th Sunday of Lent	March 17
		Palm Sunday	March 24
		Paschal Triduum	March 28
		Easter Sunday	March 31
2014	A	Ash Wednesday	March 5
		1st Sunday of Lent	March 9
		2nd Sunday of Lent	March 16
		3rd Sunday of Lent	March 23
		4th Sunday of Lent	March 30
		5th Sunday of Lent	April 6
		Palm Sunday	April 13
		Paschal Triduum	April 17
		Easter Sunday	April 20

Year	Sunday Year	Lent	Date
2015	B	Ash Wednesday	February 18
		1st Sunday of Lent	February 22
		2nd Sunday of Lent	March 1
		3rd Sunday of Lent	March 8
		4th Sunday of Lent	March 15
		5th Sunday of Lent	March 22
		Palm Sunday	March 29
		Paschal Triduum	April 2
		Easter Sunday	April 5
2016	C	Ash Wednesday	February 10
		1st Sunday of Lent	February 14
		2nd Sunday of Lent	February 21
		3rd Sunday of Lent	February 28
		4th Sunday of Lent	March 6
		5th Sunday of Lent	March 13
		Palm Sunday	March 20
		Paschal Triduum	March 24
		Easter Sunday	March 27

Year	Sunday Year	Lent	Date
2017	A	Ash Wednesday	March 1
		1st Sunday of Lent	March 5
		2nd Sunday of Lent	March 12
		3rd Sunday of Lent	March 19
		4th Sunday of Lent	March 26
		5th Sunday of Lent	April 2
		Palm Sunday	April 9
		Paschal Triduum	April 13
		Easter Sunday	April 16
2018	B	Ash Wednesday	February 14
		1st Sunday of Lent	February 18
		2nd Sunday of Lent	February 25
		3rd Sunday of Lent	March 4
		4th Sunday of Lent	March 11
		5th Sunday of Lent	March 18
		Palm Sunday	March 25
		Paschal Triduum	March 29
		Easter Sunday	April 1

Year	Sunday Year	Lent	Date
2019	C	Ash Wednesday	March 6
		1st Sunday of Lent	March 10
		2nd Sunday of Lent	March 17
		3rd Sunday of Lent	March 24
		4th Sunday of Lent	March 31
		5th Sunday of Lent	April 7
		Palm Sunday	April 14
		Paschal Triduum	April 18
		Easter Sunday	April 21
2020	A	Ash Wednesday	February 26
		1st Sunday of Lent	March 1
		2nd Sunday of Lent	March 8
		3rd Sunday of Lent	March 15
		4th Sunday of Lent	March 22
		5th Sunday of Lent	March 29
		Palm Sunday	April 5
		Paschal Triduum	April 9
		Easter Sunday	April 12

APPENDIX B:
SELECTIONS FROM THE
WRITINGS OF ST. FRANCIS DE SALES

Day	Quote	Reflection	Prayer
Ash Wednesday	LS, 3–4	LS, 2	IDL, 2:10
Thursday	OEA, 9:19	IDL, 3:35	
Friday	OEA, 8:82-3		
Saturday	LS, 80–81		OEA, 26:388f
1st Sunday A	LS, 19		LS, 32
1st Sunday B	TLG, I:150f		OEA, 26:405
1st Sunday C	LS, 19		OEA, 26:415
Monday 1	LS, 88		
Tuesday 1	OEA,26:394	OEA,26:388	OEA, 26:414
Wednesday 1	LS, 41	Exercises, 36f	
Thursday 1	OEA,26:388	TLG, II:263	OEA, 26:411
Friday 1	TLG, II:237	TLG,II:162ff	
Saturday 1	LS, 121		OEA, 26:407
2nd Sunday A	LS, 63	LS, 58–59	OEA, 26:396
2nd Sunday B	OEA,26:398	LS, 62–63	OEA, 26:395
2nd Sunday C	Camus, 153f	OEA, 9:28ff	OEA, 26:419
Monday 2	OEA,26:413	TLG, I:244ff	
Tuesday 2	OEA, 8:289		
Wednesday 2	OEA, 8:293	OEA, 8:293	
Thursday 2	IDL, 3:15		
Friday 2	OEA,13:145	OEA,13:145	
Saturday 2	OEA, 6:22	OEA,26:414	OEA, 26:392
3rd Sunday A	TLG, I:133		
3rd Sunday B	TLG, II:181	TLG, II:189f	
3rd Sunday C	OEA, 7:128		
Monday 3	IDL, 3:5		
Tuesday 3	OEA,26:412	OEA, 9:272	
Wednesday 3	OEA,12:359		
Thursday 3	Camus, 201		
Friday 3	TLG, II:170	TLG, II:171	
Saturday 3	IDL,3:28	Prayer, 14	
4th Sunday A	TLG, I:110		
4th Sunday B	LS, 179–80	OEA, 9:39ff	

4th Sunday C	*IDL, 1:11*	OEA, 2:393	
Monday 4	*TLG, I:90f*		
Tuesday 4	*TLG, I:93*	TLG, I:97	
Wednesday 4	*LS, 94–95*	OEA, 9:86-7	
Thursday 4	*OEA, 7:120*	OEA, 7:123f	
Friday 4	*OEA, 7:125*		
Saturday 4	*TLG, II:40*		
5th Sunday A	*OEA,10:312*	OEA, 8:97ff	
TLG, I:91f	*OEA, 6:22*		
5th Sunday B	*TLG, II:278*		
5th Sunday C	*OEA, 14:79*	IDL, 3:28	
Monday 5 Years A and B	*OEA, 12:251–52*		
Monday Year C	*OEA, 22:27*		OEA, 26:418
Tuesday 5	*CC, 54–55*		OEA, 26:414
Wednesday 5	*TLG, I:66*	TLG, II:277f	
Thursday 5	*OEA, 7:74*	OEA, 7:74f	
Friday 5	*OEA,26:301*		
Saturday 5	*LS, 184*	LS, 185–86	IDL, 1:17
Passion Sunday A	*LS, 171–72*	LS, 170–71	
Passion Sunday B	*LS, 21*	LS, 22–23	
Passion Sunday C	*LS, 97*	LS, 166–67	
Monday of Holy Week	*IDL, 3:14*	LS, 74–75	
Tuesday of Holy Week	*LS, 195*	LS, 192–94	
Wednesday of Holy Week	*IDL, 3:14*	LS, 191–92	
Chrism Mass	*Letters, 111*	OEA, 7:13f	
Holy Thursday	*OEA,26:211*	OEA,26:215	
Good Friday	*TLG, II:281*	TLG, II:45f	OEA, 8:429
Holy Saturday-Vigil Mass A	*TLG, II:139–40*	OEA, 10:431–33	
Holy Saturday-Vigil Mass B	IDL, 4:12	OEA, 26:229–30	
Holy Saturday-Vigil Mass C	TLG, I:251	OEA, 9:171–72	
Easter Sunday	OEA,15:101		

SUGGESTIONS FOR FURTHER READING

WORKS OF ST. FRANCIS DE SALES IN FRENCH

Oeuvres de Saint François de Sales, Edition Complète. Annecy: Monastère de la Visitation, 1892–1964. 26 volumes. Noted as *OEA.* The translations are the author's unless otherwise noted.

SUGGESTED WRITINGS OF ST. FRANCIS DE SALES

The Catholic Controversy: St. Francis de Sales' Defense of the Faith. Translated by D. Mackey. Rockford, IL: Tan, 1989. Noted as *CC.*

Francis de Sales, Jane de Chantal, Letters of Spiritual Direction. Translated by Sr. Peronne-Marie Thibert, V.H.M. Introduction by Joseph F. Power, O.S.F.S. and Wendy M. Wright. Preface by Henry J. M. Nouwen. New York: Paulist Press, 1988. Noted as *Letters.*

Francis de Sales: Selected Letters. Translated by Elisabeth Stopp. New York: Harper, 1960.

Introduction to a Devout Life. Translated with introduction by J. K. Ryan. New York: Doubleday, 1966. Noted as *IDL.*

Lenten Sermons of St. Francis de Sales. Translated by the nuns of the Visitation. Edited by Lewis Fiorelli, O.S.F.S. Rockford, IL: Tan, 1985. Noted as *LS.*

The Sermons of St. Francis de Sales on Prayer. Translated by the nuns of the Visitation. Edited by Lewis Fiorelli, O.S.F.S. Rockford, IL: Tan, 1984.

Spiritual Conferences. Translated by William Ruhl, O.S.F.S. Online at the Web site of the Oblates of St. Francis de Sales available at http://www.oblates.org/spirituality/spiritual_conferences/.

Spiritual Directory of St. Francis de Sales: Reflections for the Laity, Commentary by Lewis Fiorelli, OSFS. Boston, MA: c. 1985.

Spiritual Exercises by St. Francis de Sales. Translated and edited by William N. Dougherty, O.S.F.S. Introductory essay, notes, and bio-bibliographical note by Joseph F. Chorpenning, O.S.F.S. Toronto: Peregrina Publishing, 1993.

Treatise on the Love of God. Translated with introduction by J. K. Ryan. 2 vols. Stella Niagara, NY: De Sales Resource Center, 2007. Noted as *TLG*.

BIOGRAPHIES OF ST. FRANCIS DE SALES AND ST. JANE DE CHANTAL

Lajeunie, E. J. *Saint Francis de Sales: The Man, the Thinker, His Influence.* 2 vols. Translated by Rory O'Sullivan, O.S.F.S. Bangalore, India: SFS Publications, 1986.

Ravier, André. *Francis de Sales: Sage and Saint.* Translated by Joseph Bowler, O.S.F.S. San Francisco: Ignatius Press, 1988.

Stopp, Elisabeth. *Madame de Chantal: Portrait of a Saint.* Stella Niagara, NY: De Sales Resource Center, 2002.

SALESIAN SPIRITUALITY

Camus, Jean-Pierre. *The Spirit of St. Francis de Sales.* Edited and translated by C. F. Kelley. New York: Harper, 1952.

Ceresko, Anthony, O.S.F.S. *St. Francis de Sales and the Bible.* Bangalore, India: SFS Publications, 2005.

Chorpenning, Joseph, O.S.F.S., ed. *Human Encounter in the Salesian Tradition: Collected Essays Commemorating the 4th Centenary of the Initial Encounter of St. Francis de Sales and St. Jane de Chantal.* Rome: ICSS, 2007.

Corrignan, François. *The Spirituality of Francis de Sales: A Way of Life.* Translated by Joseph Bowler, O.S.F.S. and Lewis Fiorelli, O.S.F.S. Bangalore, India: SFS. Publications, 1992.

Dailey, Thomas, O.S.F.S. *Praying With St. Francis de Sales.* Winona, MN: St. Mary's Press, 1997.

McDonnell, Eunan, S.D.B. *God Desires You: St. Francis de Sales on Living the Gospel.* Dublin: Colombia Press, 2001.

———. *The Concept of Freedom in the Writings of St. Francis de Sales.* Berlin: Peter Lang, 2010.

Pocetto, Alexander, O.S.F.S. *The Ecclesial Dimensions of Salesian Thought.* Hyattsville, MD: Institute of Salesian Studies, 1972. Available at http://www4.desales.edu/~salesian/ecclesial.html.

Sankarathil, John, O.S.F.S. *God of the Ordinary: A Spirituality for All.* Bangalore, India: Asian Trading Co., 1999.

Stopp, Elisabeth. *A Man to Heal Differences: Essays and Talks on St. Francis de Sales.* Philadelphia: St. Joseph's University Press, 1997.

———. *Hidden in God: Essays and Talks on St. Jane Frances de Chantal.* Edited by Terence O'Reilly. Philadelphia: St. Joseph's University Press, 1999.

Wright, Wendy. *Francis de Sales: Introduction to a Devout Life and Treatise on the Love of God.* New York: Crossroads, 1993.

———. *Heart Speaks to Heart: The Salesian Tradition.* Maryknoll, NY: Orbis Books, 2004.

INTERNET
RESOURCES

De Sales Resources and Ministries Web site available at
http://www.desalesresource.org/.

De Sales Spirituality Center Web site available at
http://www.oblates.org/spirituality/.

De Sales University Web site available at www.desales.edu.

International Commission on Salesian Studies Web site available at
http://www4.desales.edu/~salesian/resources.html.

Oblates of St. Francis de Sales–International Congregation Web site
available at www.desalesoblates.org.

Oblates of St. Francis de Sales of the Wilmington-Philadelphia
Province Web site available at www.oblates.org.

Salesian Studies Web site available at
http://www.desales.edu/default.aspx?pageid=10077.

Christus Publishing, LLC Web site available at
http://www.christuspublishing.com.

COVER ART

Painting of St. Francis de Sales at the Visitation Monastery of Untermarchtal, Germany. Painter unknown, ca. 1850. Photo: Rev. Herbert Winklehner, O.S.F.S.

ABOUT THE AUTHOR

Fr. Alexander T. Pocetto, O.S.F.S. entered the Oblates of St. Francis de Sales in 1945. He obtained the A.B. degree in Philosophy as well as an M.A. in French from the Catholic University of America and was awarded the Ph.D. in French Language and Literature from the University of Laval, Quebec. He did his theological studies at the De Sales School of Theology in Hyattsville, Maryland and was ordained in 1955. Fr. Pocetto spent the first ten years of his priesthood as a high school teacher and administrator. For the past forty-five years, he has been at De Sales University in Center Valley, Pennsylvania, where he was a founding member and served in various capacities including positions as a member of the French faculty, Academic Dean, Vice President for Academic Affairs, Acting President, and Senior Vice President.

He currently teaches a course in Salesian Spirituality and holds the position of Senior Salesian Scholar in the Salesian Center for Faith and Culture at De Sales University. He has served on the Provincial Council of the Wilmington-Philadelphia Province and on the General Council and held the position as Assistant Superior General of the Oblates of St. Francis de Sales. In 1992 he was appointed Chairman of the Congregation's International Commission on Salesian Studies

(ICSS) and served in this capacity for twelve years. He was instrumental in setting up the ICSS's first website.

His doctoral thesis dealt with the relationship of St. Francis de Sales and the independent thinkers of his day. Over the years, Fr. Pocetto has published articles in a number of periodicals such as *Salesian Studies, Review for Religious, Journal of Indian Spirituality, Salesianum, Proceedings of the Patristics, Medieval and Renaissance (PMR) Conference, Jahrbuch für Salesianische Studien, (Yearbook of Salesian Studies)*, as well as essays in several books specifically dealing with Salesian spirituality. He has published a book on the history of De Sales University stressing its Oblate-Salesian roots and mission and edited several others. Over the years, he has given parish missions, numerous retreats to both priests, religious and lay people on Salesian themes. A number of his articles and/or conferences are available online at http://www.desales.edu/default.aspx?pageid=10077#Pocetto.